THE
RELIGIOUS CASE
AGAINST BELIEF

THE
RELIGIOUS
CASE
AGAINST
BELIEF

JAMES P. CARSE

THE PENGUIN PRESS

New York | 2008

THE PENGUIN PRESS
Published by the Penguin Group • Penguin Group (USA) Inc., 375 Hudson Street,
New York, New York 10014, U.S.A. • Penguin Group (Canada), 90 Eglinton Avenue East,
Suite 700, Toronto, Ontario, Canada M4P 2Y3 (a division of Pearson Penguin
Canada Inc.) • Penguin Books Ltd, 80 Strand, London WC2R 0RL, England •
Penguin Ireland, 25 St. Stephen's Green, Dublin 2, Ireland (a division of Penguin
Books Ltd) • Penguin Books Australia Ltd, 250 Camberwell Road, Camberwell,
Victoria 3124, Australia (a division of Pearson Australia Group Pty Ltd) • Penguin Books
India Pvt Ltd, 11 Community Centre, Panchsheel Park, New Delhi–110 017, India •
Penguin Group (NZ), 67 Apollo Drive, Rosedale, North Shore 0632, New Zealand
(a division of Pearson New Zealand Ltd) • Penguin Books (South Africa) (Pty) Ltd,
24 Sturdee Avenue, Rosebank, Johannesburg 2196, South Africa

Penguin Books Ltd, Registered Offices:
80 Strand, London WC2R 0RL, England

First published in 2008 by The Penguin Press,
a member of Penguin Group (USA) Inc.

1   3   5   7   9   10   8   6   4   2

Copyright © James P. Carse, 2008
All rights reserved

"I heard a fly buzz when I died" from *The Poems of Emily Dickinson: Variorum Edition*,
Ralph W. Franklin, ed., Cambridge, Mass.: The Belknap Press of Harvard University Press.
Copyright © 1998 by the President and Fellows of Harvard College. Copyright © 1951,
1955, 1979, 1983 by the President and Fellows of Harvard College.

LIBRARY OF CONGRESS CATALOGING IN PUBLICATION DATA
Carse, James P.
The religious case against belief / James P. Carse.
p.   cm.
ISBN 978-1-59420-169-1
Includes bibliographical references (p.   ) and index.
1. Religion—Philosophy.   2. Faith and reason.   I. Title.
BL51.C37   2008
200—dc22   2008010217

Printed in the United States of America
Designed by Marysarah Quinn

For Tom F. Driver

If God held all truth in his right hand and in his left the everlasting striving after truth, so that I could always and everlastingly be mistaken, and said to me, "Choose," with humility I would pick the left hand and say, "Father, grant me that. Absolute truth is for thee alone."

—GOTTHOLD EPHRAIM LESSING

To believe is to know that one believes, and to know that one believes is no longer to believe.

—JEAN-PAUL SARTRE

God said it. I believe it. End of discussion.

—BUMPER STICKER

CONTENTS

INTRODUCTION

Why a *religious* case against belief?

In the current and quite popular assessment of religion, there is one thing conspicuously missing: religion itself. It has long been a fashion, and even more so now, to frame arguments against religion in largely scientific language. From that perspective critics are right to expose the inherent falsehood of much that believers claim to be true. The popular argument states that those who do believe in God, or Allah, have fallen "under a spell" worked on them by clever but fraudulent thinkers. Or that religious belief was once useful to the evolution of human culture but is now an impediment to mature societal advance. What is more, believers are not just wrong; they are also dangerous. Here, too, critics have abundant material to target. So-called true believers—those so convinced of the rectitude of their convictions they are eager to die, or to kill, for them—have brought once inconceivable havoc to the human community. Even a cursory glance at the present conflicts across the globe, executed in the name of religion, seems to justify a twist on the traditional Islamic exclamation, asserting that God is *not* good.

For all of their righteous passion, however, what these critics are attacking is not religion, but a hasty caricature of it. Religion has presented itself in so broad an array of disconnected and unique manifestations across the span of human history that no generalization can conceivably apply to the full variety of its expression. Although the critics in question are for the most part accomplished students of both science and modern society, their interest in the subject of religion seems to have been exhausted by a few initial glances at the actions of several selected groups of avid believers. This is a misfortune. Considering the extent of the chaos attributable to it, a reflective and religiously literate critique of belief is a necessity.

Offering a religious case against belief obviously implies that religion is not strictly a matter of belief. It may come as a surprise that a thoughtful survey of the history of religion provides scant evidence for an extended overlap of the two. Quite simply, being a believer does not in itself make one religious; being religious does not require that one be a believer. This improbable distinction has been hidden by the tenacious notion that religion is chiefly a collection of beliefs. By this account, Hindus have a certain catalogue of assertions to which one must assent in order to take the name for oneself, Jews another. This leads to the absurd perception that one could, for example, come to a full understanding of what it means to be a Jew by carefully listing everything Jews are thought to "believe."

But if a religion is not strictly a matter of believing, what is it? Take note first of the irreconcilable differences between the historic religions. Although Islam and Christianity have been close neighbors for a full fourteen centuries, it is unthinkable that Muslims might occasionally mistake themselves for Christians. There is something in each tradition that definitively sets it off from the other. But what? It might seem reasonable at this point to consult Christians to learn what their religion is at its core, then turn to Muslims with the same request. After the first few inquiries, we would discover that there is little agreement within Christianity and within Islam as to how the core of each faith is to be articulated. Indeed, this is such an open question that both traditions largely consist in the struggle over what it means to be a Muslim or a Christian. At the center of each, in other words, is a mystery they cannot fully comprehend; neither can they cease attempting to comprehend it. They may give this mystery the name "God" or "Brahman" or "Tao," but when we ask for more complete clarification, agreement among them scatters. How then can we say what the Christian religion *is* when Christians themselves have never been able to do so?

Yes, an inclusive definition of religion is out of reach, but to acknowledge that is not to terminate meaningful discussion of the issue. Instead, we must integrate the factor of unknowability into each of our conceptions of religion. This can have a strong effect on our thinking in general: reflecting on the remarkable way the great religions seem to develop an awareness of the unknown keen enough to hold its most ardent followers in a state of wonder, we may begin to acquire the art of seeing the unknown everywhere, especially at the heart of our most emphatic certainties. This is not just to develop a new intellectual talent, but to enter into a new mode of being, a "higher ignorance."

Through higher ignorance, an open-ended dialogue becomes possible. It is the goal of this book to reach beyond the phenomenon of belief not merely to defend the religions but to discover how higher ignorance can inform our most ordinary experience. Far from being a critical failure of religion, valued in this way higher ignorance is the beginning of wisdom.

Why a religious case against *belief?*

In one respect, it is not a mistake to associate religion with belief. Mystery is difficult to live with, and for some even terrifying. It can often be of great comfort to hide our unknowing behind the veil of a well-articulated belief system. For this reason, the historic religions seem to be a particularly fertile source for absolutisms. But when "true" believers claim that their convictions have been validated by a given religion, they are patently unaware that in doing so they have just rejected it. The certainties that led Christians to the Crusades, or Hindus to the universal imposition of a caste system, or Muslims to truck bombs all constitute a repression of the tradition they claim as their own. What is more, belief systems or ideologies that originate elsewhere—Nazism, Maoism, Serbian nationalism, American triumphalism—present themselves as the equivalent of religion, often taking on its presumed trappings: Nazi ritual, Mao's Little Red Book, the demarcation of sacred soil, the mission of democracy to enlighten a corrupted world.

This should be enough to indicate that the act of belief is highly complicated and richly nuanced behavior. That it consists of an avowed commitment to a set of truth-claims is the least part of it. On closer analysis in the following chapters, we will find that, among other features, belief thrives on conflict, depends on

INTRODUCTION

the clarity and restricting power of its surrounding boundaries, has a one-dimensional understanding of authority, possesses a kind of atemporality that denies any possibility of an open history, and builds on a severe form of self-rejection. These are characteristics of belief rarely cited in the general discussion. They appear in sharp profile only when we consider their inherent hostility to religion.

In sum, to counterpoise religion and belief is to make possible a deeper insight into both. Given the violence that originates in the absolutism of belief systems, it is urgent that we come to a more incisive grasp of what is at stake. It is proper to hold belief systems to the most stringent canons of knowledge in all its forms. In the process, however, we must take care not to pitch knowledge against religion, as though one is the violation of the other, for in truth they are in essential harmony. The challenge is not to make religion intelligible but to use knowledge religiously. Aristotle wrote that knowledge begins in wonder. By thoughtfully assessing the unmatched vitality of the great religions, we can begin to see that knowledge also ends in wonder.

PART I
BELIEF

Summoned to Rome in 1633, the aged and ailing Galileo Galilei made the arduous journey from Florence carried on a litter through mostly dreadful weather. He was, however, confident that the Inquisition would conclude in his favor. He had reasons for thinking so. Pope Urban VIII had been a firm champion of his work and once had even written an ode in his honor. He was at the pinnacle of his scientific career. Although his discoveries had been received with some controversy, especially in the church, he had admirers at all levels of the hierarchy. He was probably the most famous person in all of Europe. Before his death he would be visited by a parade of notables, including Thomas Hobbes and John Milton. He regarded the trial largely a nuisance, a costly interruption of his work. What is more, it seemed highly improbable that the pope would make himself a fool in the estimate of the intellectual world. Galileo was nonetheless aware that there were powerful people outraged by his ideas. He knew as well that the outcome of every Inquisition was unpredictable. And in the background, there was always the possibility, however remote, of torture and prison, common features of an ecclesiastical trial.

The Inquisition, as history cannot forget, did not bear out his confidence. After months of interrogation, the exhausted, seventy-year-old Galileo gave in to the demands of the papal officers and signed his famous "abjuration." Specifically ordered to reject Copernicus's theory that the "earth is not the center of the universe," he agreed it was false and swore never to teach it again. The statement he was then forced, or chose, to sign is stark. Its decisive sentence leaves little ambiguity: "With sincere heart and unfeigned faith, I abjure, curse and detest my errors." And then, as if this were not enough, he added the disturbing promise, "Should I know any heretic or person suspected of heresy, I shall denounce him to this Holy Office."[1] The confession, extreme as it was, softened but did not prevent his punishment. He was exiled to his farm in the village of Arcetri, near Florence, where he was held under virtual house arrest for the remaining eight years of his life.

The common view of this notorious event is that it demonstrates the inevitable conflict between religion and science: on the one side is a set of fixed beliefs, resistant to the slightest modification; on the other is the open and free inquiry into the nature of the physical world. But there are several problems with this view. For one thing, Copernicus, a Polish monk, published his *De Revolutionibus* a full ninety years before Galileo's trial. Not only was he not censured for these findings, they had been largely unchallenged by both the church and the scientific community. In fact, they had become an unexceptional ingredient in the general discourse among scholars in such great universities as Padua, Bologna, Oxford, and Paris. For another, nowhere in the transcript of the trial nor in the many volumes of his published work is there any suggestion that Galileo questioned the church's authority in matters of faith, as Luther had a century earlier. On the contrary, he repeatedly professed his devotion to the Holy Mother Church, even after his abuse at the hands of her inquisitors. What sense are we to make of this perplexing event?

Part of the answer lies in the fact that Galileo accepted the authority of the church *in matters of faith*. This authority did not, however, extend to *matters of science*, that is, *knowledge*. The two remain distinct throughout his writings. For him, neither the church nor the scriptures claimed as the source of its doctrine had anything to add to or correct in the findings of his experiments. But this went in both directions: if church doctrine had no role in judging the accuracy of scientific research, science offered no basis for the improvement or rejection of belief. The phases of Venus had no theological significance; the Bible was silent on the velocity of falling objects.

There is a deeper issue at play in the long saga of the church's struggle with Galileo. He was passionate about finding the truth of all things physical. He sometimes spoke as if we could assemble a catalogue of empirical observations that would account for all of the mysteries of the material universe. But the actual course of his life tells us something else. Consider that he did not merely count the moons of Jupiter with his telescope and leave it at that; he made thousands of observations, always improving the manner of doing so, all the while taking careful notes. He may have been determined to find the truth of the motion of the planet's moons, but he never gave up on attempting to discover what was yet unknown about them. He accepted nothing as a settled conclusion. Aristotle's reasonable teaching that objects of different weight fall at different speeds typically inflamed his contrariness. It was not enough to prove Aristotle wrong. He went on to write a long treatise, *De Motu*, on the laws of motion, after years of experiment and calculation. Even then he held back publication for years more, uncertain he was not mistaken in a few details. Galileo was dedicated to the truth however it emerged. But what we see in his life is that there is no end of truths, and not one of them beyond challenge. There is always something new and unexpected to be learned. What drove him, in other words, was not his knowledge but his ignorance. He *knew* that he did not know. He also knew he never would know it all.

To associate Galileo with ignorance may seem a bit odd. It is important, therefore, to have a precise understanding of what is involved in making this connection. The word "ignorance" can be understood in at least three very different ways. In the first, and simplest, it indicates a lack of knowledge of one kind or another. For this, the term *ordinary ignorance* will do. We do not know who will win the next election, what the weather is in China, or whether marriage to this person will work out. It is important to note that in principle we can satisfy these bits of ignorance with intelligible information. All of us are ignorant in this way. Indeed, there is no end of things that we do not and will never know, but could understand were we apprised of them. In one respect ordinary ignorance is a trivial phenomenon. It does, however, have larger consequences when the object of our ignorance is of danger to ourselves or others: an undetected virus, faulty automobile brakes, hidden behavioral motives.

The second form of ignorance is subtler and potentially far more dangerous. Call it *willful ignorance*. It is a paradoxical condition in which we are aware there is something we do not know, but choose *not* to know it. It is assuming an ignorance when there is no ignorance. I avoid asking what a friend truly thinks of me, though it is perfectly evident there are strong feelings involved. We are aware that our teenage children have a full world outside our own, but we deliberately shield ourselves from it. Creationists act as if they are oblivious to the huge and tumultuous field of evolutionary theory. In its more menacing form, we can expect to find it in political oppression, the making of war, the recruitment of suicide bombers, the uneven distribution of wealth, inasmuch as we cannot be involved in any of these activities and be unaware of what we are doing—but act as if we are. If the fighter pilot focuses on the devastating effect of his rockets, it will most certainly reduce his effectiveness, so he deliberately keeps his attention on the electronic signals that indicate only where and when he is to activate the weapons. The rich will often make a conscious choice to shield themselves from the circumstances of the poor; there are matters there that they would rather not know.

A particularly apt example of willful ignorance is the debate over the personhood of a fetus. So-called right-to-life ideologies claim scientific support for their belief that personhood begins at the moment of conception. That may well be true about personhood, but there can be no *scientific* support for the notion. Anyone who is even faintly familiar with scientific methodology knows perfectly well that not only the beginning, but the entire phenomenon of personhood—indeed, life itself—falls well outside the capacities of science. It is in this sense that those who firmly believe that personhood begins at conception are willfully ignorant: they intentionally overlook the great mass of scientific work that leaves that question unanswerable. To call on scientific authority in this case is a false gesture, and they know it. The same point can be made for their opponents. If the right-to-life ideology has no objective ground for its claims, neither does the "freedom of choice" ideology. If there is no justifiable claim that personhood begins at conception, neither can there be such a claim for the beginning of personhood later in pregnancy. The attribution of personhood at *any* stage in life has no scientific justification. Neither party therefore has science on its side; both have nothing more than their beliefs. The debate cannot be resolved, and should not be.

There is a third kind of ignorance so different from the first two that it seems not to deserve the name at all. Although it is found at the heart of the philosophical and religious traditions from their earliest appearance, there is no simple way to define it. I will refer to it as *higher ignorance*. It is this kind of ignorance that describes the inner dynamic of Galileo's life work. Although he himself never directly refers to his work in this way, it would not be surprising had he done so. He was certainly familiar with a then famous essay, written about two centuries earlier: *De Docta Ignorantia* (Concerning Learned Ignorance) by Nicholas of Cusa (1401–64). Nicholas was an astronomer, mathematician, theologian, and philosopher, a polymath of such talent that he is often singled out as the most brilliant mind of the fifteenth century, a figure not unlike that of Galileo himself. Nicholas puts the matter with typical elegance: "Every inquiry proceeds by means of a comparative relation," he writes, "whether an easy or a difficult one. Hence, the infinite, qua infinite, is unknown; for it escapes all comparative relation."[2] By "comparative relation," Nicholas means simply the way one finite thing can be related to another. No matter how many of these relations we might perceive, they will never add up to the infinite. Thus our ignorance of what things *truly* are. Truth, after all, is not only infinite, "but is something indivisible. . . . Hence, the intellect, which is not truth, never comprehends truth so precisely that truth cannot be comprehended infinitely more precisely." No matter how many *truths* we may accumulate, our knowledge falls infinitely short of *the* truth.

In a New Testament verse well known to Nicholas, the Apostle Paul tells unbelievers on the Areopagus in Athens that his God is that one "in whom we live and move and have our being." This is not a god that can be viewed from without, and therefore cannot be known except through our partial experience of it. In Thornton Wilder's *Our Town,* a character speaks of a letter addressed to "Jane Crofutt; The Crofutt Farm; Grover's Corners; Sutton County; New Hampshire; the United States of America; Western Hemisphere; the Earth; the Solar System; the Universe; the Mind of God."[3] Everything has an address somewhere *within* the universe, except for the universe itself. Where, after all, is the mind of God? Although at first the Crofutt farm, a concrete and earthly reality, seems to have its own place in the settled order of things, when we are told that the universe has a location unknown to us, there is no saying where the farm *really* is: here, and also nowhere. Indeed, the entire population of Grover's Corners did not know where they really were; they were alive and yet they were also dead. Wilder makes this point by looking outward at the increasingly vast context in which we find ourselves. We can turn just as easily in the other direction. What could be closer to us, for example, than our own consciousness? While the attempt to explain the phenomenon is compelling, it is doomed by the fact that the explanation in itself can proceed only from within a state of consciousness. For what lies outside, we cannot even formulate a meaningful question. How could we be conscious of something we are not conscious of? Here, too, we have nothing more to say than that our consciousness is where we live and move and have our being.

Nicholas was at pains to show that higher ignorance understood this way is not the kind of unknowing we are born with. Neither is it the same as Socrates' ironic claim to ignorance, inasmuch as it was a kind of trick that lead others into intellectual dead ends or contradictions, and therefore is a variety of willful ignorance. Nor is it the common truism that the more we know, the more we see what we do not know. This is but a form of ordinary ignorance. By stressing that it can only be *learned*, higher ignorance comes only as the result of long reflection, combining a deep reading of the thinkers who have gone before us with a continuing process of self-examination. The Latin word *docta* in Nicholas's title is a variation on the Greek *doxa*, or teaching. We must be taught to be ignorant.

Ignorance thus described can be understood as a process of *awakening*, or of being awakened. The more we are aware of the limitations of our knowledge, the more awake we are to the world's enormous varieties. At the risk of stretching the metaphor too far, ordinary ignorance is a sleep that does not know itself as sleep—like Wilder's characters, dead but unaware they are dead. The willfully ignorant are in a state of wakefulness, but one that feigns sleep, intentionally restricting the horizon of their daylight world. Nicholas's learned ignorant are awake, and know they are awake, but also know they will never succeed in altogether dispelling the unwanted drowsiness.

By asserting an equivalence of learning and ignorance, Nicholas has provided a convenient lens through which we can identify a stream of thought familiar to a wide variety of thinkers in every age and tradition. The residents of Plato's cave, for example, could see only shadows, and even when they left the cave they could look directly at the source of light only with difficulty. The Roman philosopher Plotinus spoke of the real as One; the only way we could observe it is to be separate from it, and to be separate from the One is to pluralize it, in which case it is not the One we are observing. Plotinus, though a pagan, had a strong impact on medieval thought and especially the Jewish, Christian, and Islamic mystics. To know God, they typically said, is to be God; therefore, not being God, all things divine remain forever hidden from us. We can follow this line of thought even up to the modern period. Kant taught that since we cannot know a thing as it is in itself, the ultimate nature of the world is finally inaccessible to the rational mind. Nietzsche scoffed at the very idea of objective knowledge, declaring that it is only the result of creative thinkers and not a representation of anything. Heidegger wrote that the question no thoughtful person can avoid—why is there something rather than nothing?—is perfectly unanswerable. Freud, too, belongs to this abbreviated list, inasmuch as he said of the id—that enigmatic reservoir of repressed thoughts and desires—that it is timeless, chaotic, and all but permanently concealed from the conscious ego.

But awakened ignorance has its most natural home in the great religions, and is by no means limited to Christianity. (Nicholas was that rare medieval thinker whose curiosity ran to all philosophies and religions.) Enlightenment for the Buddha, for example, is impossible without the suspension of the speculative mind. Even then, once achieved, the elevation to ever higher levels of purified mindfulness never ends. Brahman, the sublime deity of Hinduism, is so transcendent that it cannot be defined except to say it is "not this and not that" (*neti neti*). According to the Tao te Ching, life is a journey that stops nowhere and is of no permanence. The repeated phrase of Muslims, "by the will of Allah," reflects an awareness that there is no predicting what that will may be. The rabbinical tradition in Judaism is a discourse of many thousands of voices, but a discourse in which no one has the final word.

When emphasizing ignorance in our understanding of Galileo's life and thought, it is essential not to confuse one kind of ignorance with another. His life project was to rid the world of its *ordinary* ignorance. And indeed he was enormously successful in doing so. Not only did he solve questions that had long been pondered (the displacement of water, for example, by objects of different weight), he discovered features of physical reality no one had thought to inquire into. Not a living soul ever wondered if the circumlocutions of the Earth could be proved by calculating the phases of Venus, or whether after a descent of two seconds a falling body has acquired twice the speed it had at one second.[4] Although these are mysteries of a kind, they are of a smaller order, and they all are soluble. Urban VIII was not troubled by ignorance of this kind. What he evidently sensed in Galileo was an ignorance that nothing can erase, a permanent unknowing.

From his side, Galileo evidently sensed in the pope and his inquisitors an ignorance of a very different kind. His opponents were on the whole intelligent enough to understand what he was about in his numerous experiments, but they explicitly chose not to expose themselves to it. After discovering the moons of Jupiter, he invited his skeptical colleagues on the faculty at the University of Padua to look through his telescope themselves. Some of them refused outright, knowing that nothing less than their assiduously acquired Aristotelian understanding of the world was at stake. Some did look but incredibly reported that they saw no moons. Galileo made no secret of his discoveries. He published his calculations. The phenomena he described were already in plain view. If they were not noticed, it can only be that the viewer decided not to notice them, even while looking directly at them. How else to describe this but as an act of *willful* ignorance?

It was neither ordinary nor willful ignorance on Galileo's part that led the church to such drastic action against him, but what has been described as *higher* ignorance. It shows itself most obviously in his indefatigable curiosity, an inquisitive search for new truths, a search made possible only by learning the depth of his own ignorance. It is to be noted that Galileo presented most of his important theories in discursive form, through three characters, two of whom (Salviati and Sangredo) were actual persons, recently deceased. The third, Simplicio, a kind of fictional naif, never quite understood what was being discussed. The pope (wrongly) thought Simplicio was a caricature of His Eminence. In fact, it is more likely that he was a voice of Galileo's own, as Socrates was for Plato. At one point Simplicio sighs, "When shall I cease from wondering?" Giorgio de Santillana, in his brilliant study of Galileo's life and thought, suggested that this could be a motto for all of his work.[5] In other words, if it were not for Simplicio's persistent ignorance, these famous dialogues could not have been written. Galileo's inquisitors, on the other hand, were not *inquisitive* at all. No ignorance there, much less wondering. They had all of the answers before a single question was asked. How could they not be alarmed by his genius at finding questions at the heart of the most certain of answers?

Of course, Galileo's questioning did not cease with his abjuration. Predictably, even after he was confined to his farm in the Tuscan hills, he wrote what many consider his most important work, *Discourses and Mathematical Demonstrations Concerning the Two New Sciences*. His works were all condemned and often burned in public places, but he nonetheless managed to smuggle the book to Leyden, where it was published in 1638, three years before his death.

History has not forgotten Galileo's condemnation by Urban VIII but it has all but completely forgotten Urban VIII. In his time, the pope was a man of great earthly power. In fact, for fully twenty years of his papacy he was actively engaged as a principal force in the Thirty Years War, which like most wars was ideologically driven, unnecessary, and exceedingly destructive to all sides. It was a war, let us remember, of believer against believer. The pope's effect on his enemies was enormous. Galileo, with no legions of his own, had but a negligible effect on the pope. But his effect on the history of civilization cannot be exaggerated. He is therefore a model not of cowardly capitulation, but of the distinctive encounter between belief and wonder. The encounter, however, is not one of opposition. He did not *defeat* Urban and his formidable *ecclesia*. He did something far more significant: he exposed their willful ignorance. The old man who sat before the inquisitors was a living reminder of the mysteries that gave the Christian tradition its religious power. To acknowledge this they would have to admit that their precisely stated beliefs had no durable substance, but were arbitrary inventions that falsely claimed the quest for truth had been completed. By declaring Galileo a heretic they painted themselves with that very brush.

The importance of this for us in the twentieth and twenty-first centuries should be obvious. We have seen consequences of the destructive power of belief that far exceed those of a certain seventeenth-century church hierarchy. Belief systems (or ideologies) held with the same fervor in our own age have had, and continue to have, horrors unimaginable to Galileo's contemporaries. His inquisitors were not exactly suicide bombers but they held their views with the same intensity. Torture, long terms of imprisonment in appalling conditions, and death by the most painful means possible were the recommended treatment of unbelievers, even those who deviated but slightly from the standards of orthodoxy. (In Galileo's youth, the great astronomer and philosopher Giordano Bruno, found guilty of theories resembling his own, was burned alive in the central piazza of Florence, an event that he could well have witnessed.) The pope's Thirty Years War was a horror, but it hardly compares to Stalin's starvation of the kulaks and Mao's Cultural Revolution, and certainly not to the unspeakable crimes of the Holocaust. For true believers, it is a short distance from the seventeenth century to the twenty-first.

The word "belief" has as many uses and varied meanings as "ignorance." It reaches across a wide range of content and intensity. We can arrange beliefs on a scale that begins with the casual, little more than mere asides or guesswork. At the opposite end are beliefs that we live and die for, or kill for. At the soft end of the continuum would be those that come in the form of such expressions as "I do believe the weather is improving," or "We've got to believe that the planet Earth is in a stage of acute warming." In each case, we are indicating that there is something we do not yet know but are inclined to suppose is the case. Beliefs at this level may be concerned with something relatively insignificant (the weather) or with something of great importance (global warming) but are not held with such ardor that we would defend them on pain of death.

As we move along the continuum, these same beliefs can take on greater consequence for our own actions. Believing in global warming, we may decide to make extensive changes in our use of natural resources—to give up the use of a car or seek to live exclusively by renewable energy sources. We may choose even more vigorous actions, such as joining social protests and physically resisting the destruction of forests or wetlands. If, on the other hand, we believe that global warming is a fiction promoted by certain antisocial elements, we might more actively promote the consumption of petrochemicals and support police action against disruptive environmentalists.

Note that the *content* of our beliefs does not in itself determine where we locate them on a scale of intensity. I may believe that God created the world in a week, but have no interest in what the schools are teaching children. For the same belief, I might chain myself to the doors at the Board of Education and refuse all food and legal assistance until God is firmly installed in the curriculum. What seems trivial to one believer may produce anguish and vital challenges to another.

The metaphor of the continuum is chosen to indicate that the kind of belief that concerns us here stands at the far end of the scale of passion and action. At this point believers have crossed the line from uncertainty to conviction. There is no possibility of a reasonable objection. Those who disagree are placed in the category of unbelief and can therefore be bracketed out of serious conversation. So our attention shifts away from cataloguing beliefs according to their content, arranging and assessing them for what they seem to claim—their truth-value—to the deeper structure of belief itself. What are we doing when we *really* believe, that is, strongly enough to put our life—and the lives of others—in acute jeopardy?

Before we turn to the task of defining belief, there is a bit of confusing terminology to be cleared up: the distinction between "belief" and "faith." Do they represent different forms of belief, or do they refer to the same phenomenon? Confusion between the two terms arises from the fact that in the Greek text of the New Testament there is only one word for both (n. *pistis*, v. *pisteuein*). In Latin there are two related words, *credere* and *fides* (roots of such English words as "credit" and "fidelity"). But because one is a verb and the other a noun, their usage is difficult to compare. Moreover, the issue of belief is primarily a Christian phenomenon. Christianity is a religion always busy defining what its worshipers should be thinking. But belief is not only a Christian phenomenon, especially when we are dealing with belief *systems*, and belief systems can occur anywhere. To simplify my use of the terminology, I will employ the two words as follows: so long as we are concerned with belief systems, I will use the term "belief." I will reserve the use of the term "faith" for the more complicated discussion of religion itself. As briefly as possible, Maoism and Panslavism are belief systems, Christianity and Islam are faiths (albeit spawning any number of belief systems). It is unnecessary to define the terms more closely here; the distinction between them will emerge as the discussion continues.

The twelfth and thirteenth centuries are usually referred to as the Age of Faith. It was a time of expanding scholarship in both Christianity and Judaism, as well as Islam. It was also a time of war. More than six Crusades took place in those years.[6] But for all the religious ardor of the Age of Faith, it doesn't compare to the explosive spread of belief and its power in the present age. We are seeing what could fittingly be called a second Age of Faith.

Statistics tell some of the story. Assorted polls indicate that as many as eighty-five percent of Americans describe themselves as believers. Fifty percent say they are regular churchgoers. As many as seventy-five million Americans claim to be "born again" Christians. Although membership in the mainline Protestant and Catholic churches is showing some weakness, the pentecostal and evangelical denominations are expanding at an extraordinary rate. While both Reform and Conservative synagogues continue to be strong, Orthodox Judaism has never seen such growth. Mormonism, first appearing a century and a half ago, is arguably the fastest-growing body of believers in history. Publication of religious books is unprecedented. The "Left Behind" books—a twelve-volume fictional account of Armaggedon, the final battle in which Jesus takes unchallenged command of the world—are one of the most successful publishing ventures in religion, ever. The Bible has been translated into several thousand languages with countless more planned.

By no means is the Age of Faith II restricted to America. In the last several decades evangelical Christianity has swept through Central and South America with breathtaking speed. Orthodox Christianity has seen a dynamic rebirth in Russia. Christians in South Korea will soon make up half the country's population, and boast enthusiastically that they intend to convert all of Asia in this century. Hinduism has seen a dramatic rise in fervor with a profound effect on Indian social and public life. Islam is adding new members at rates never seen in its fourteen-hundred-year history, and on every continent. There is a measurable ebbing of religious belief in Europe, particularly in the state-supported churches, but Europe is clearly out of step with the rest of the world.

These are just the numerical indicators. More significant is the remarkable extent to which issues of faith have penetrated public and political life, particularly in Asia, the Islamic countries, and America. Three recent American presidents—Carter, Clinton, and George W. Bush—have repeatedly declared themselves to be "born again." Without accepting Jesus as one's "Lord and savior," or at least one's "favorite philosopher," it is difficult to be elected to public office. There is a widespread and well-organized effort to enact legislation that agrees with a number of sectarian beliefs. The constitutional separation of church and state has become, for the first time in American history, an area of intense debate. One prominent American public figure accuses the "secular Left" of conducting an "unending war against God in America's public life." This is a "Christian country," he adds, "endowed by God."[7]

The (Christian) faith of the American founders has been emphasized as never before. Even the Supreme Court has been the subject of intense religious attention, especially among conservative Christians, giving support to a theory of interpretation of the Constitution called "originalism," one that strongly resembles a "literalist" interpretation of the Bible.[8]

But if the first Age of Faith had an appetite for war, Age of Faith II far outdoes it. The Crusades are repeating themselves with vastly greater deadliness. Every major conflict on earth involves the collision of one belief with another. Examples come quickly to mind: Hindus and Muslims in India; Christians and Muslims in Nigeria; the Falun Gong in China; Christianity and Islam in the Middle East; Israelis and Palestinians; Muslims and Christians in the Sudan, as well as Kosovo, Chechnya, and even France,

Denmark, and Holland. If we consider Nazism and Marxism, along with scores of nationalisms, as pseudo-religious belief systems (as we shall see, there are good reasons to do so), the history of the past hundred years is one of all but unimaginable bloodshed between bodies of believers. Less grave than warfare, though avidly engaged, are debates over abortion, theories of evolution, homosexuality, same-sex marriage, even polygamy—all of them populated with committed believers.

The emergence of Age of Faith II has rightly attracted a broad army of critics. It has, in fact, become fashionable to assail religion for its excesses—and for the excesses of the ideologies that reach the level of religious intensity. The question is how effective these critics have been, and how appropriate their objections are.

Two recent attempts, both passionate and both determinedly scientific, can be cited. In the first, Sam Harris's *The End of Faith*,[9] the author asserts in sizzling prose that "religion is nothing but bad concepts held in place of good ones for all time. It is the denial, at once full of hope and full of fear, of the vastitude [*sic*] of human ignorance."[10] The concepts are "bad" for at least two reasons: they are simply false—on strictly factual grounds—and they repeatedly lead their believers to violence. Islam, referred to as the "House of War," comes in for a special drubbing.[11] "On almost every page, the Koran instructs observant Muslims to despise nonbelievers," preparing the ground for "religious conflict."[12] For the author, we will be rescued from the evils of religion only by universal scientific education. Nothing, he writes, "is more sacred than facts."[13] Except for the resistance of ignorant believers, this is not a particularly difficult task: "an utter revolution in our thinking could be accomplished in a single generation: if parents and teachers would merely give honest answers to the questions of every child."[14]

Harris's assumption is that religious belief is a matter of "historical and metaphysical propositions." A companion work by a popular writer of science, Daniel Dennett,[15] agrees, and adds that we can show empirically that religious belief has evolved in a roughly Darwinian manner, by causes so natural they can be explained by the physical sciences. From its primitive origins it has so concentrated and refined itself that it now holds billions of believers in its "spell," caught by attachment to such unrealities as God, the soul, and life after death. Religion, he says, is the most powerful force on earth, therefore the most dangerous. Here, too, the author attacks religious beliefs, however they evolved, as false claims. And the solution is the same: universal scientific education, the only way of "breaking the spell."

There are several fatal problems with such a treatment of religion. The most obvious is the presumption that the errors and evils of religion can be eliminated by the kind of verifiable information suitable to the classroom and laboratory. Belief systems are stunningly resistant to such correction, for the simple reason that deeply committed believers are not offering a variety of debatable proposals about the nature of the world. They see the world *through* their beliefs, not their beliefs from a worldly perspective. Therefore, whatever happens can only confirm the truth of what they believe. When we present believers with contrary "evidence," we only prove to them that we are outside the realm of faith and therefore unable to see the world as it is. For this reason, belief systems are not only impervious to opposition, they thrive on it. Such arguments can only defeat themselves. Objections of this kind come dangerously close to being belief systems themselves. They have the presumption of being able to explain everything. Working scientists, viewed within the context of their study, presume nothing of the kind. In fact, the sciences are populated with a huge crowd of brawling, non-monolithic thinkers. It is disagreement, not agreement, that keeps scientific passion at its keenest. One person's conclusion is an invitation to another's challenge. Authorities are faced with unruly and skeptical rebels. The scientific enterprise has, in fact, a close similarity to the rabbinical tradition: what has previously been taught is considered an advance over its predecessors, but the duty of every student is first to learn what has been taught, then to question it, then to succeed it. The process does not pretend to be headed toward consensus or any kind of conclusion. (The New York Public Library lists in its own catalogue more than forty-five hundred scientific journals, nearly all of which can be read and understood only by scholars in the corresponding fields.) Scientific activity in this sense has a strong quality of disputation, one that has nothing to do with questions like belief in God—in fact, one that has nothing to do with belief at all. There is, therefore, considerable irony in the strategy of holding believers to the standards of empirical, or scientific, knowledge. Neither of our authors seems to note that his critique edges over into a belief system of its own.

Also, although they are scientists of impressive credentials, Harris and Dennett seem not to have noted that if we live in the

Age of Faith II, we also live in the Age of Science. Almost five centuries have passed since the great astronomers began rearranging the universe, exposing the errors of traditional beliefs by empirical observation and mathematical calculation. If religious belief were vulnerable to objective, scientific analysis, it would have sagged, if not crumpled, under the cascade of factual knowledge that followed. In fact, the opposite has occurred. In the first decades of the last century, Germany had achieved a general level of education the world had never seen. Its universities were famous for scholarly brilliance. The sciences were strongly encouraged and heavily subsidized by the state; so were literature, film, painting, and theater. Nonetheless, the intellectual and professional classes, no less than the working class, rushed with patriotic fervor into a belief system that led to a previously unthinkable mass crime and a world war. Marx spent years in the British Museum accumulating mountains of fact to support a theory that was to transform half the world into believers so convinced of its truth that they would sacrifice as many as a hundred million lives to prove it. The Soviet Union became a world power by way of extraordinary scientific achievement in all fields, especially weaponry. It even replaced religion in school and university curricula with science courses. Plenty of facts, but considering their use, hardly "sacred." Marxist and Nazi believers transformed the world—in a few years—like no one before. By comparison, Islam's "House of War" is a mere footnote in the modern history of scientifically underwritten savagery. During this time, the historic religions have only increased in participants, often exponentially. Reason is not a solution to religion's errors, not a cure for the violence that continues in its name. In fact, it is hard not to conclude that science and religion, far from excluding each other, act as reciprocal stimuli. This is not to say that scientists are becoming more religious but that in the presence, or under the assault, of science, believers have become more emphatic and more incorrigible. We need observe nothing more than the virulent reaction of believers to the scientific theories of evolution and natural history—theories that rise from mountains of incontestable fact.

A second error in the usual attack on religious belief is to assume that there exists some one thing that can be called religion. Contrary to the naïve claim that at bottom "all religions are the same," there are countless religions and pseudo-religions so distinct from one another that almost no generalizations about them can be made. Attempts to define religion as a unitary phenomenon are famously unsuccessful. Characteristically, attacks on religion tend to overlook the vast and uneven detail in this tapestry, reducing it to a cartoon drawn only as a fitting target for ridicule. Because of this, depictions of the religion under attack by even its most sophisticated and passionate unbelievers are never recognized by its believers as an image of their own. Proving the nonexistence of god is an especially embarrassing exercise. Any student of religion would ask immediately, Which god is it exactly that you are disproving? Typically, the god unbelievers are rejecting is one found nowhere within the living religions.

A third and the most damaging flaw in the customary critique of religion is the failure to distinguish between the religions themselves and the belief systems with which they are often identified. For example, there is a belief system (actually a number of them) that can be called Christianity. At the same time, there is a Christianity that is emphatically not a belief system, one that finds itself in a long tradition, long enough to pre-date Jesus himself. This may seem an odd claim since Christians are constantly at work laying out orthodoxies (scores of them) and drawing up creeds (hundreds of them) to settle disputes concerning which beliefs are correct and which heretical. It is notable that not one of these creeds has succeeded in permanently closing down debate over proper belief; they have not succeeded because there is a deeper vitality in the Christian faith, as in all the great religions, that no single belief system can fully represent.

That there is no tidy match between religion and belief systems is obvious in the fact that some religions are all but free of beliefs (Buddhism and Judaism, for example), and in the further fact that there are belief systems (Fascism and Marxism) that can hardly be considered religions—although it makes sense to consider them pseudo-religions.

It should be apparent that we are concerned here not with isolated and disconnected beliefs but with belief *systems*—comprehensive networks of tenets that reach into every area of thought and action. Well-developed belief systems have the capacity to account for and explain any issue or question that might arise. They present themselves as thoroughly rational and comprehensible, while answering to a final authority, whether that be a person or a text or an institution. But they are not only large intellectual schemes. They often have distinctive historical narratives, an extensive mythology, a pronounced sense of community, a pantheon of heroes and martyrs, an array of symbols, scripted rituals, sacred geographical sites and monuments. On top of all this is an absolute certainty in the truth of their beliefs. What is more, they see themselves surrounded by treacherous unbelievers who wish nothing but their demise. Nazism and Marxism contain all of these features, from such definitive texts as *Mein Kampf* and *Das Kapital* to symbols like the swastika and the hammer and sickle. There is no event in the past or present that does not fit neatly into their ideology. Comradeship, heroism, blood bonds, a supreme authority, the universal validity of their truths, ethnic purity, a dangerous circle of enemies—it is all there. They present a tidy, accessible, and coherent view of the world complete with an ethic for dealing with it. They have succeeded in cleansing the thinking of their believers of all mystery. Everything makes sense. The assorted belief systems within both Christianity and Islam, though most definitely distinct from those of the Soviets and Nazis, share each of these components. So do the countless nationalisms and ethnic movements that continue to cause such widespread social distress.

Contrasting religion with belief systems seems to indicate an absolute difference, with a clear line between them, black and white. This is, of course, not the case. There are belief systems that have strong elements of religion in them, and there are religions that frequently come close to recasting themselves as belief systems. I will keep the distinction as I have drawn it only to simplify the discussion. Moreover, using Marxism and Nazism as examples may seem to suggest that all belief systems are uniformly dangerous, or worse. Belief systems run the full range from all-out evil to the trivial and harmless.

A belief system that is presented in graceful, nonantagonistic language, also learned and reasonable, is Richard John Neuhaus's *Catholic Matters* (New York, 2006). About his conversion from the Lutheran to the Catholic Church, Neuhaus speaks of "becoming the Catholic I always was" (chapter 2). The church for him was always there; it was in no need of him to discover it, for it is anchored in the reality of God and preserved through history by the action of the Holy Spirit. To be obedient to the central teaching of the church, or Magisterium, is to be in direct contact with Christ who is "coterminous" with the church. Because the New Testament was communicated directly by Christ through the apostles and the Catholic tradition, it bears the truth in its fullness, and is therefore not "just a message dropped into the maelstrom of history" that anyone can interpret as they like. The authority of the church is above question. Its Magisterium "to some extent patrols the outer boundaries of the permissable, and occasionally disciplines egregious offenders" (p. 104). In no way can Neuhaus be directly associated with the evils of the preceding century, but the inner logic of belief systems is on full display in this work.

So far as we preserve a distinction between belief systems and religion, it should become clear that the vast, organized, and savage criminality of the last one hundred years or more is the result not of religion, but of belief. One could argue, of course, that the Russian Revolution of 1917 was a reaction to the repressive policies of the tsars. But in fact, while the great majority of Russians had lived in appalling conditions for centuries, it was not until there appeared a new and dazzling complex of ideas that collective action against tsarist rule was possible. The Russian Revolution was initially an intellectual protest. It was the creation of educated bourgeois and even some aristocrats. The ensuing crimes were committed not by undisciplined mobs but by genuine believers. The same can be said for Nazism. Hitler was a virtual unknown until the publication of a *book*. His *Mein Kampf* laid out an all-embracing scheme of ideas that quickly made believers of millions. It may not be too much to say that *all* modern revolutions, beginning with the French, are idea-driven.

The ideology of the French Revolution was so complete that it not only reconceived the role of the government but even rearranged the calendar, changing the name and dating of days, months, and years. The tragedy of the revolution is that the iron certainty of its believers led them from the ideal of equality to the runaway horrors of persecution and punishment. The American Revolution, also a creation of highly educated upper-class gentlemen, had a different outcome because of a simple but profound intellectual insight: they developed a belief system that did not completely believe in itself. By conscious design, they left holes in it, creating space for new ideas and social realities, and all but invited constant redefinition—reflected most obviously in a separation of powers able to check each other. Ironically, although many Americans want to underscore the (Christian) beliefs of the founding fathers, what gives the United States its distinctive identity is its ability to restrain the excesses of belief—of all kinds. We easily speak of the "idea of America," an often unaware acknowledgment that it is not a fixed political entity but an accidental community of persons whose collective identity is under the constant recreation of its *thinkers*. (Does it make sense to speak of the "idea" of Germany, or Zambia, or China?)

The point is simply this: belief systems are exceedingly powerful, able to gather a unified body of dedicated persons for explicit political action, regardless of their physical, social, and cultural circumstances. And unless they do not have internal checks against the absolutism of their own beliefs, the power of their shared belief is aggressively directed at the unbelieving and hostile world around them.

Although some of the world's most developed religions may contain any number of belief systems within themselves (Shia and Sunni in Islam; Orthodox, Catholic, Protestant, and evangelical in Christianity), these systems cannot comprehend or contain the religions in which they locate themselves. The religions are simply not reducible to tidy formulas or rigidly ordered credos. No limits or definitions can be imposed on them, nor can they be the exclusive possession of a single community. Unlike belief systems, they are not at their core intelligible, and they are saturated with paradox. A careful study of the religions will reveal a dynamic capacity to change, to grow, and to expand—but *without losing their identity as this religion or that.* Let the religions produce what belief systems they may. The belief systems, however, cannot produce a religion (though a great many have tried).

The best way to dissect the inner structure of impassioned belief is to examine a prominent example. We can hardly do better than Martin Luther's appearance before Charles V, the Holy Roman Emperor, when he defied the emperor's demand that he recant his false beliefs. The example is especially attractive for it contains elements of raw bravery, deep learning, and enormous consequences: it not only led to a deep division of Christendom, but had a far-ranging influence on the structure of modern thought. At the same time, the example also exposes the dangers and the inner contradictions of the phenomenon of belief. It is an oft-cited instance of religious courage; almost never, however, is it seen as an example of the alarming flaws of belief.

On April 19, 1521, Martin Luther entered the city of Worms, standing in a two-wheeled cart pulled by a common farm horse. He had been summoned to appear before Charles for what was in effect a heresy trial. Charles had strong reasons for confronting Luther, then a monk of the Augustinian order. Four years earlier, in an act of ecclesiastical defiance, Luther had nailed to the door of the cathedral at Wittenberg, where he was a professor of theology, ninety-five theses attacking the spiritual authority of the Church of Rome. Although he was completely unknown to the larger world, copies of his theses swept through Europe in months, aided by the recently invented printing press. In fact, in that short period of time Luther's fame had grown so rapidly that although he chose to enter Worms in this modest conveyance, he was accompanied by two thousand loudly vocal supporters. The emperor, rightly alarmed that the young monk's irreverence had the power of rending the Christendom he was divinely appointed to rule, had taken the extreme step of ordering Luther to appear in person and account for his teachings.

The proceedings opened with an examination of Luther's writings, still a rather modest collection of documents, by learned emissaries of the pope. They quickly and definitively proved his errors. He was commanded to recant. He hesitated, asking for time to prepare his response. It was clear, however, that his mind had been made up. He had earlier written to a friend, "This shall be my recantation at Worms: 'Previously I said the Pope is the Vicar of Christ. I recant. Now I say the Pope is the adversary of Christ and apostle of the devil.' "[16] Returning two days later, he made his famous declaration: "I will recant nothing. Here I stand, I cannot do otherwise."[17]

The emperor was predictably furious. He allowed Luther to leave the city under the safe conduct he had previously promised him, but on May 6 the Edict of Worms was published, leaving little doubt as to the emperor's conclusion: "This devil in the habit of a monk has brought together ancient errors into one stinking puddle and has invented new ones. . . . Luther is to be regarded as a convicted heretic. When the time is up, no one is to harbor him. His followers are also to be condemned. His books are to be eradicated from the memory of man."[18]

Luther was promptly excommunicated. His response was characteristic of the spirit of the trial: "As they excommunicated me for the sacrilege of heresy, so I excommunicate them in the name of the sacred truth of God. Christ will judge whose excommunication will stand."[19]

It is not surprising that the unprotected, diminutive figure, scarcely five feet tall and weighing less than a hundred pounds, fearless before an emperor who commanded armies, is a vivid image in Christian history. It is an iconic example of the true believer, ready to pay any price for what he knows is the truth. The emperor was right, Luther was a danger to the realm and to the faith; but so was the emperor a danger to Luther. These were two powerful men facing each other across a line neither of them would cross. Charles remained untouched by the young monk's teachings. The monk never retreated. Each held to his beliefs without a hint of compromise. Luther's defiant bravery, even insolence, put him at severe risk, but it also left the emperor temporarily helpless. All of his tools of persuasion had been disabled. Not torture, not death, not even excommunication were credible threats. Nothing would change the young man's thinking. For that reason, it was the defenseless who had the greater power. Shortly after Luther left Worms, the emperor sent soldiers to kill him but, under the protection of Frederick the Wise, Elector of Saxony and a partisan of the reformer, he escaped to Frederick's castle at Wartburg where he spent nearly a year in hiding.

Luther's conduct before the Holy Roman Emperor is a model of true belief inasmuch as he knew exactly where he stood, was certain of the truth, then drew a line around it, a line he refused to cross. So it is for other believers; they "take a stand," they "hold to what they believe," they "defend their position," they "keep their ground," repelling the inevitable challenge from nonbelievers. The image is familiar and universal: persons armed with nothing more than their convictions facing hostile and dangerous opponents of superior worldly power. Christian history is heavily populated with martyrs who gladly died for their faith; so are the histories of other religions and countless ideologies. Nonetheless, the example is disturbing for a number of reasons. Can we find a nationalism that does not memorialize and celebrate its martyrs?

A deeper look into Luther's trial and his response to the emperor reveals a number of features of belief that go far beyond a simple exchange of opinion, even if it causes a hostile, dangerous encounter. First, consider the fact that both Luther and the emperor worshiped the same God, read the same Bible, were raised in the same church, and that their faith was refined by the same great thinkers in Christian history. Their beliefs in *these* matters were never an issue in the trial. Indeed, they were not even enumerated or discussed. The only beliefs that counted were those that stood in opposition to each other. It wasn't just that Luther believed the pope had no special authority in matters of faith; it was that Charles (along with the pope and the full weight of Christian doctrine) had precisely the contrary belief that made their encounter necessary. In fact, if they had agreed on this subject, or if the emperor had been indifferent to the issue, the trial would not have been held and we would have heard nothing about their views of the pope. There would have been no mention of this belief at all; it would not even have appeared to be a belief. In other words, the act of belief is always an act *against*; it requires an opponent who holds the contrary belief.

This feature of belief is hardly limited to Christianity. How could there be Sunni Muslims if there were no Shia? Would Israeli settlers have been so vocal in declaring G-d's promise concerning the land of Judaea and Samaria if Palestinians had not thought it was they to whom it belonged? Could American patriots have flourished during the cold war in the absence of their Soviet counterparts?

Belief systems thrive in circumstances of collision. They are energized by their opposites. For every believer there is a nonbeliever on whom the believer is focused, whose resistance is carefully delineated. We could go so far as to say that belief is so dependent on the hostile other that it may need to stimulate the other's active resistance. Belief has a confrontational element built into itself that is essential to its own vitality. If believers need to inspire fellow believers to hold firmly to their position, they need just as much to inspire nonbelievers to hold to theirs. For this reason, belief systems are territorial. They stand off from all others and rarely do they overlap. (Note how often countries go to war, or threaten war, over disputed boundaries— Kosovo, Taiwan, and "Kurdistan," for example, or for that matter the American Civil War.) They act variously as factions, states, blocs, interest groups, parties, ethnicities, and schools of thought. Each of these has its comprehensive network of beliefs that offers a thorough analysis and assessment of itself and its opponents. Even self-defined ethnic groups have more than just a (presumed) shared genetic heritage; they have developed a convincing characterization of their persecutors, and they have elaborate explanations for their superiority or purity and detailed histories that justify it all. Just as they share with most other varieties of belief systems a panoply of heroes and martyrs, sacred sites, scriptural texts, and binding rituals, their rivals fall under similar but reversed characterizations. They are schismatics, breakaway groups, racists, apostates, fallen backsliders, subversives, false ideologues, forces of evil, aggrandizing powers, intolerant majorities, all of whom are dedicated to the repression and destruction of one's own group of believers. They are in every respect *other*, but in this case a hostile other.

Second, because belief is always belief against, it is itself an act of unbelief. It is the active refusal to take a rival position. To believe something, one must disbelieve something. Each belief must not only have an opponent; it must have an opponent whose (dis)beliefs are a perfect match. For this reason, each is largely *defined by its opposite.* If beliefs die when their opposition disappears, they are obliged to mimic any changes the opposition makes of itself. Belief and unbelief are therefore locked into mutual self-creation. Imagine that Luther, under the urging of the emperor and the attending theologians, shrugged his shoulders and said, "Fine. I can alter my position to accord with yours." Should they still be determined to call him a heretic, they must then search out a new issue over which they can nourish their rejection of each other. Failing that, whatever the content or the intensity of their beliefs, the act of believing becomes meaningless. The consequences would have been significant. Not only would the issue have died; the historic Christian church may well have stayed intact. To be sure, there were other "reformers" than Luther, but when the Church of Rome convened the Council of Trent (1545–1563), it was an explicit rejection of Luther's teachings that shaped the church's understanding of itself. It was only then that Christendom divided into "Catholics" and "Protestants." While one seeks the destruction of the other, it also serves to instruct the other. What better example can we offer than the way that the great belief systems of our age have painstakingly elaborated a portrait of their rivals. The Nazis presented a detailed account of the worldwide domination of "Jewish bankers" whose only goal was the economic subjugation of the rest of the earth. Radical Muslim sects have an almost farcical view of the "Zionist" program against Islam. In the United

States, radical underground military groups find evidence everywhere that the government is developing a hidden counterforce to steal their freedoms. Conspiracy theories often operate in the conflicted encounter of belief systems. In American politics the opposing parties are as much antiliberal and anticonservative as they are liberal and conservative. Even a Supreme Court justice, Antonin Scalia, dissenting in a case that rejected the Texas law forbidding sodomy, referred to what he called "the homosexual agenda."

The point I want to stress here is that in this case we have gone far beyond mere disagreement, even beyond outright collision; *both sides depend on each other to know what they believe.* They are joined in a kind of compact that freezes them to a stable self-understanding consisting of a reverse image of the other. There is no middle ground, no dialogue that could result in modified doctrine and practice.

An instructive instance of the belief/unbelief compact is the French Revolution. At the beginning, the *sans-culottes* knew exactly what they were up to—because they were energetically opposed by a royalty and nobility whose thinking and policy had broad unanimity, at least as they saw it. As the revolution proceeded, its success in destroying the opposition caused it to lose an instructive contrast to itself. With a desperate hunger to understand what it was about, it began wildly hunting for anyone who resisted, including some whose loyalty was beyond question, even the revolution's principal figure, Robespierre himself. In the end the destroyers destroyed themselves. As a belief system its coherence and appeal disappeared. The idea of revolution had a powerful resonance around the world, but the ideas of the revolution itself had so lost their distinctiveness that there was no way either to believe or to disbelieve them.

A third way that the drama in the cathedral at Worms illustrates the phenomenon of belief lies in the fact that it was an affair of highly learned men. Young Luther had already shown commanding scholarly talent; the emperor himself was both devout and a passable student of doctrine; present in the assembled company was a stable of Christendom's most powerful intellectual forces; there was no shortage of knowledge or subtlety of thought; every one of them was thoroughly multilingual. These remarkable facts should make us wonder why they so passionately resisted each other's arguments, finding not the merest patch of common ground. It obviously cannot be that there is a division in knowledge itself. Because their educations were identical, it can only be a division between knowers. What else can we say but that they chose not to think what their opponents were thinking? Here then is a trenchant clue to understanding our subject: *belief marks the line at which our thinking stops,* or, perhaps better, the place where we confine our thinking to a carefully delineated region. Maoists or creationists or jihadists or libertarians take a severely critical view of the world, but they do not step across their created boundaries to take an equally severe view of themselves.

Believers stop their thinking at a designated line only when they refuse to see their shared dependence with disbelievers. They do this even though at some level they are aware that they are doing it—a classic act of willful ignorance. Only by being willfully ignorant do we not acknowledge that, as believers, we have drawn real dialogue with others to a halt. Each of our beliefs is shielded against the damaging scrutiny of others—and ourselves. We have passed from a conversational to a declarative mode. We have nothing more to say to one another about our beliefs except to announce and defend them. The young Luther, a manifestly brilliant thinker, let his thinking go only so far. But so did his examiners. Both sides knew perfectly well that they had drawn the boundary line in tandem, but the line could hold only if they did not step across it to look back at themselves from another perspective. As in a student debating contest, they could have switched sides and ably argued each other's position—but by doing so they would have necessarily opened their thinking to new possibilities. In other words, *they invented a division within a shared knowledge that need not exist.* They were certainly intelligent enough to think the thoughts of the other, but it was precisely this that they refused to do.

Because this admittedly uncommon definition of belief is so important to the remainder of the book, it is appropriate to look more deeply into the importance for believers to curb their thinking. In his first letter to the Corinthians, Paul addresses their concern about eating meat offered to idols (8:1–13). His view is that knowing, as they should, that the gods represented by the idols do not exist, eating the sacrificed meat is harmless; however, they should be careful not to do so in the presence of those who think the idols are potent, for it would only increase their false knowledge. In other words, the danger lies not in the idols themselves but in how the Corinthians *think* about them. To this somewhat benign example, we can cite others much darker. U.S. laws against the desecration of the flag make the same error in reverse: they transfer to the physical object the reality for which it is only a symbol. Therefore, by protecting the material on which the designs are stamped, we protect the ideas "for which it stands." When the Taliban destroyed historic statues of the Buddha, when the Nazis burned Jewish books, when Muslims cover the flesh of women in dark clothing, it is dangerous *thinking* that was their target. The Buddha speaks in his first sermon of "right thinking." In some Buddhist meditation disciplines, one is to let thoughts "pass by," that meditators might free themselves from attachment to them. In one of the most severe remarks attributed to Jesus is the injunction, "If your right eye offends you, cut it out," a clear warning not to think libidinous thoughts. American captors of presumed terrorists have learned that tearing pages from the Quran in the face of its believers is an effective insult to the captives' "way of thinking." In each of these cases, it is not the object but the thinking associated with it that is at issue. There is no greater danger to belief than "false" thinking. The line must be absolutely clear.

By defining belief as the point where we bring our thinking to an end, I by no means intend to claim that believing means the end of thinking altogether. On the contrary, believers *must* be thinkers. Belief absent of thought is not belief at all, only a habit of mind, or empty repetition. What is critical here is not that belief cancels thinking altogether but that it requires a decision to confine it to a carefully inscribed region. While covering a woman with a burka may prevent certain thoughts, it can nonetheless be demanded by profound thinkers. Within the realm of belief, there is no end to the possible depth and reach of thoughtful reflection—as long as it is *within*. What lies beyond must remain beyond. If the act of belief does not have the power of containing our thinking within those boundaries, it is not belief. After all, one cannot believe everything. There must be limits. If not to think at all is a habit of mind, to believe anything we want is an emptying of mind; in both cases it is meaningless to speak of belief. The boundary then defines an arena in which our thinking is free to wander, and in which it *must* wander—but only so far.

What then are we to say about the nature of that boundary? Back to Luther and the emperor, we note that each of them takes refuge in an *authority*. For the emperor, it is sacred scripture and the whole body of Christian doctrine—as the pope interprets them; for Luther, it is sacred scripture and the whole body of Christian doctrine—as he interprets them. What may escape our attention in this battle is that they both *choose* their authorities. No authority was imposed on them. In fact, one of the issues in the conflict is that by citing himself as a sufficient authority to interpret scripture, Luther implicitly challenges the emperor to notice that he has the same freedom as Luther. Were Charles to acknowledge this self-evident fact, the encounter between the two of them would have been between only the two of them; the church, along with its leaders, teachers, and scholars, would then have played no role at all. The two believers could have met in a local tavern and clarified their differences, or come to fisticuffs over them, with no large implications for any other believers.

The rude fact here is that Charles called down the authority of the institution, then stood behind it to condemn Luther. By virtue of his immense military and political power, he was free not to assign definitive authority to the pope, or the church, or the scholars assembled in the cathedral, though he did so.

The case with Luther is more complicated, and more revealing of the full nature of belief. Yes, he declared himself faithful to his idiosyncratic reading of scripture, as if it were all the authority he needed, but we know something else about him that puts that declaration in a different light. The anonymous knights of Frederick the Wise who rescued Luther as he left Worms took him to Frederick's castle at Wartburg. There, over the year he was hidden from the emperor, he spent most of his time in a small cell translating the Bible from Hebrew and Greek (and, incidentally, establishing his dialect as the formal German language). One dark night during this "exile," as he thought of it, he was so disturbed by the temptation to deny God that he felt the active presence of Satan, whom he tried to drive off by throwing an inkwell at the demon's shadow—leaving a stain on the wall some claim is still visible. But the splattered ink never completely covered over Luther's struggle with himself. That he never escaped these deep misgivings is evident in the frequent reference in his later writings to temptation (Ger. *Anfechtung*), or the desire to turn away from God. A powerful contradiction took hold of his self-understanding. He described himself as *simul justus et peccator*, at the same time justified and a sinner. Moreover, he became increasingly skeptical of rationality in understanding spiritual matters, even calling reason a "harlot." He was, in fact, drawn to a mode of thought that draws itself into question. "When I am told that God became man," he typically remarked, "I can follow the idea, but I just do not understand what it means. For what man, if left to his natural promptings, if he were God, would humble himself to lie in the feedbox of a donkey or to hang upon a cross?"[20] The apparently defiant Luther of the trial, we know now, had a more formidable opponent even than the emperor—himself. A man of prodigious intellectual energy, his struggle was not with the Church of Rome, but with his own inquisitive, restless mind. The only way he could settle on a final catalogue of beliefs was to fight back the other Luther who continued to question and to wonder, a struggle he only partly won.[21]

What this reveals about the nature of belief is perhaps obvious: stopping our thinking at a publicly designated limit is not only a response to some external power or danger, but also to an internal danger, one that far outweighs all others. The internal danger is our desire both to construct a barrier around ourselves *and* to breach it. This is no doubt the most naked appearance of the contradiction that lies at the heart of the act of belief. Whatever the content of our beliefs—be they Lacanian deconstructionism, Marxist feminism, Wahabi jihadism, or Sartrean nihilism—they all are an act of limitation against the nonbeliever without and the nonbeliever within. In other words, as believers, *we are in fact acting against ourselves*; we are caught up in a mode of self-rejection.

It is precisely from this point, incidentally, that we can trace another of Luther's influences on modern thought. Kierkegaard's strong sense of the self divided against itself, and the anxiety that is thus created, derives directly from Luther, whose work he carefully studied. Anxiety and self-loathing are dominant features of the works of Nietzsche (a Lutheran pastor's son), so too those of Heidegger (once a Catholic seminarian), and of Sartre (grandnephew of Albert Schweitzer). Freud, in his theories of the warring, largely hidden forces that shape the individual psyche, and even civilization itself, echoes the same insight. Indeed, it is impossible to find any area of modern thinking, from political theory to the theater of the absurd, where some trace of the stain of Luther's ink cannot be detected.

Luther, therefore, has a double legacy. By his defiant act of belief, a display of certainty in the cathedral at Worms, Christianity split into two great divisions, giving rise to a long history of social, political, and cultural strife, then split again, and again, into an unknown number of denominations and sects. Warfare and persecution flourished like malignant fungi within the divisions that belief created. On the other hand, the existential lack of certainty that assailed him as he bent over his books in an unheated cell in the dismal castle at Warburg was an opening into a profound revolution in philosophical and psychological thought, where belief was displaced by a fiercely unrestricted inquiry into our need for and use of belief.[22]

Learned as they were, it is evident that the antagonists at Worms were not simply sparring with each other over one or two isolated beliefs. On each side there was a fully developed and comprehensive way of viewing and interpreting the world. Even though a few beliefs may have found agreement across the divide, it was nonetheless a collision between two irreconcilable perspectives on almost *everything*: their respective methods of reading scripture, their attitude toward papal authority, as well as their conception of the religious life including the place of clergy in it, the sacraments, the relation of church to temporal authority, even their views of history. *And yet*, all of these differences are found within the larger phenomenon of Christianity itself. However thorough and learned their belief systems were, neither was large enough to be considered a final and definitive delineation of the faith—even though each intended it be such. As noted, each of these systems is but one of countless others that are contained within the larger religion. Indeed, such views rise and fall, disappear and sometimes reappear, with great frequency throughout the entire twenty centuries of Christianity, beginning with the New Testament.

There have been repeated attempts to capture one or another religion within one or another belief system through all of human history—monarchism, tribalism, assorted nationalisms, and any number of ethnic and political cults. The most notorious contemporary example is Nazism's striking success of folding German Christianity—Protestant and Catholic—into itself. Hitler's brilliant strategy was to interpret Christian doctrine back to believers as if it were a belief system. Believers were happy to see it so; it meant a sudden prosperity for the church through generous governmental support and exultant patriotism. Only a fraction of the church saw what was happening and dissented, sometimes at great personal cost. The high ride of the so-called Deutsche Christen, or Nazi-friendly Christians, lasted hardly a decade. Identified as they were with the Nazi Party, and without a separate identity of their own, they ended the day the party, and its war, ended. The profound withering of German Christianity that resulted continues to the present. Soviet leaders, acutely aware of the danger of independent religious activity, nationalized a few seminaries, closed others, and appointed politically loyal priests and bishops. More ambitious than the Germans, they established secular holidays and rituals to take the place of those of the church, and taught a strict atheism in the schools. Both Nazis and Soviets saw the necessity of representing religion as a coherent and intelligible whole that had its place *within* the ideology. (Note that both the German swastika and the Soviet hammer and sickle are in the shape of a cross.) How else can we explain the strange fact that the minuscule, decidedly pacifistic, and independent Falun Gong seems to have terrified Chinese leadership? The mere fact that someone is free of its ideology, or the official belief system, is a potent reminder to the nation that Maoism (however it has been refined) is *only* an ideology, one among many, therefore neither universal nor absolute. Such dread experienced by enormously powerful regimes is a clear hint that religion carries within itself a critique of all belief systems.

The salient fact that the radical break between Luther and the Roman church did not create two Christianities, that such divisions can occur without destroying the essential identity of the faith, is evidence of its remarkable vitality. In other words, that this event occurs *within* the religion is proof sufficient that *Christianity is not a belief system.* Just what it is cannot be said with satisfaction to everyone. All attempts to say what it is will find no end of dissenters. Indeed, it largely consists of an attempt to decide what it is. Christianity then is not only not to be understood by its detractors; even more, it is not to be understood by its own believers.

Here then is what we have learned from the archetypal act of belief as we find it in the encounter between Luther and the emperor: (1) While belief has its content (in believing there is always *something* believed) it is directed both inward at its faithful and outward at its opponents. (2) Moreover, its vitality depends on that opposition; in fact, the content of belief is shaped in conflict with others; were it not for this conflict we would not know what we believe. We are therefore as much nonbelievers as we are believers. (3) Because belief depends on hostile others, it is necessary for us as believers *not to think what the others are thinking,* else it could pull us across the defined boundary into another system of belief. So we must be careful to know exactly where to stop our thinking. (4) The fact that we stop our thinking at specified limits is hidden in the assumption that we are in agreement with an established authority, not seeing that it is we who have established that authority. (5) But at the same time, the very fact that we *must* set a limit to our thinking implies that we are tempted to go beyond the limits, that there is even a longing to believe the opposite. Indeed, the more passionately we hold to our beliefs, the more we are tempted to abandon them. Thus at the core of every belief is an act of self-denial, even self-rejection. (6) Because our beliefs make sense only in a complete system, and because religion is demonstrably not a belief system, and because belief systems are inherently intelligible, we are not only unable to interpret a religion as a belief system, we are not able completely to understand a religion at all. In sum, *belief is a thoroughly contradictory phenomenon.* Like the mythic serpent, the Ouroboros, belief consumes itself even as it gives birth to itself. As the discussion continues, this contradiction will steadily reappear.

First, I must acknowledge that there is a substantial objection to the phenomenon of belief as described. Unless this objection is sufficiently dealt with, the description, and the critique, will lose much of its plausibility. To remind the reader, this is a critique of belief as it is found in its most extreme forms, for which one is prepared to die, as Luther, or to kill, as the emperor. Moreover, it is a critique that has not to do with the truth or falsehood of any particular beliefs. We could go so far as to say that even if our beliefs are true, because they are *beliefs* they are still contradictory—and irreligious. Of course, what lies beyond the discussion of this objection is the task of offering a convincing understanding of the essential importance of ignorance to religion.

The objection to be addressed is simple and powerful. To put it in ordinary religious language, "I have faith because God led me to it." Or, in its more ideological form, "I believe because it suddenly came to me out of nowhere," or even "I considered the facts and suddenly saw the truth." Belief, presented this way, is not a voluntary choice. It does not originate with the believer and is not the creation of imagination or reasoning. The testimony of believers repeatedly suggests that they did not find their own way to what they believe, but were led to it, as in the familiar phrase, "I was lost, and now am found." The term "conversion" contains a distinctly passive element: believers do not convert, they are converted. Paul (then Saul), for example, was confronted by the famous vision of the risen Christ on the way to Damascus, whither he was bound to capture Christians and bring them to prison in Jerusalem. "A light from heaven flashed around him. He fell to the ground and heard a voice saying to him, 'Saul, Saul, why do you persecute me?' "[23] Saint Augustine (354–430), a giant of Christian thought, made repeated attempts to believe but was unable to "will his will" to do so until he heard an anonymous child's voice in a neighboring garden utter two simple words: "Lift" and "Look." He took up a Bible lying on the table before him and opened it at random, coming on Paul's exhortation to "give up lust and obscenity" and "clothe yourself in Jesus Christ the Lord, leaving no further allowance for fleshly desires."[24] It was as though it was not his will but that of an unknown other that led him to faith. Any number of examples could be provided to make the same point. Christian history is rich with them. So are other religions. Muhammad did not *choose* to encounter the angel Michael. Abraham was *called* out of the land of his fathers. Moses was *sent* to the mountain. The expression "chosen people" is quite fitting. As for the Buddha, it was only when he lay down under the Bodhi tree, having given up his long struggle to find spiritual peace, that enlightenment came to him, as it were, on its own. Joseph Smith did not search for a holy text inscribed on golden tablets but was *presented* it by the angel Moroni.

Thinking of themselves as converts, *chosen* to be believers by a source outside themselves, not only accords with a great deal of testimony and biography, but also opens another window into the nature of belief systems. All of the examples cited have in common the experience of making a sudden transition from one belief system to another, and not merely a new or interesting idea. It involves both an acceptance of what is revealed and a rejection of what is being left, confirming that belief characteristically takes a form of believing *against*. Add to this the common testimony that conversion by a previously unrecognized authority has the quality of being saved. This, of course, can only exaggerate the dangers of the beliefs from which we have been rescued, and thus our passionate opposition to them. Paul did not simply give up his Judaism as useless or irrelevant, he became its scourge. A conspicuous group of American thinkers and activists have thrown over their once liberal political views and have converted to a self-described "neoconservatism," determined to expose the treacherous falsehoods of what they had once believed.

To be sure, the transition from one belief system to another may not always be dramatic, and belief systems vary greatly in the intensity of their opposition. Whigs and Tories, though animated in their rejection of each other, are of a different order from Islam's Shiites and Sunnis. Their encounter is politely tempered, but the line between them is just as clear and their disagreements are just as complete.

There are at least two decisive flaws in this defense of belief. The first is that as a result of this way of thinking, *belief is raised to the status of knowledge*. Since the transition from one belief system to another is not taken on a whim, but comes unannounced and sudden, as new believers we are convinced we are coming into a realm of truth—hard, undeniable fact. One of history's most notable converts, Marx, had his awakening while reading Hegel's analysis of the master/servant relation in the opening section of *The Phenomenology of Mind*. Although he tinkered with some of Hegel's terminology (converting "dialectical idealism" to "dialectical materialism," for example), he was quickly persuaded that he had come upon the laws that shape all of human behavior—as if it were Reality making itself known.

Muslims like to say that the angels do not believe in Allah—they don't need to; being in his constant presence, they can see him directly. The implication is that they know the truth not only of divine things but of all things exactly as they are. Since we cannot see as the angels see, everything we look at, even if it is demonstrably real, is at best a shadow of the truth. To take the next step, to claim that we are in full possession of the truth, is to put ourselves in the place of angels—without noticing that we passed from knowledge (angelic) to belief (human). In this sense, Marx is the perfect model of believer. He refused to see that when he had correctly divined the laws of history, he had far overreached what knowledge genuinely gained would allow him, and conveniently ignored that these laws were the substance of belief. Like all believers, the truth was revealed to him; he did not invent it. More than that: he thought that his ideas were themselves a product of the laws of history. It was these very laws that brought Marx to an understanding of those laws. He was *chosen* by history itself to be the thinker through whom history could complete itself. This is certainty of an extraordinary magnitude. It was the assumption that no matter how others might experience the flow of history, or analyze its logic, they could do so only according to the process he alone had been chosen to present to the world.

So it is with all "true" believers. If I *know* that what I believe is true, it is as true for everyone as it is for me. Along with certitude comes universality. As some Christians put it, "If Christ is Lord at all, he is the Lord of all." If you believe something else, you are in error and must be corrected. For Marx, those who ignore the laws of history are in violation of those laws and must be brought to obey them, even if it requires massive and violent force. For some Muslims, all of those who are not followers of Allah are enemies of Allah and must be treated as such. For an American president in wartime, "Those who are not for us are against us." The tablets the angel Moroni presented to Joseph Smith were not for him alone, but for all humans both living and dead, thus the necessity for Mormons to walk the earth to announce the truth to those still in error.

The universal truth of belief is a problem especially awkward for Christians. What do we say about those millions who were born before Jesus, or those to whom his name and importance is unknown? Must they be considered, and therefore dealt with, as sinners? Some theologians have stretched the limits of Christian thought to designate certain pagan thinkers as unaware Christians. Some found Plato, for example, so compatible that they even made reference to Saint Socrates. Thomas Aquinas, vexed by the issue, came to think that full knowledge of Jesus was not necessary for those to whom he had not preached; a bare belief in the existence of God would do. Using the term *fides implicitas,* implicit faith, he proposed that those who had a genuine sense of the divine were unaware believers in Christ, since the very concept of God implied that he would be triune and that his son would be incarnate. Other religions have a similar difficulty, but different solutions. A popular belief of Muslims is that Allah created along with everything else all the souls who would ever live. Each in fact clamors to be chosen for birth. But once they have been incarnated, all memory of their eternal creation is lost. Somewhere in themselves does the truth exist in its purity, but their worldly involvements block a clear view of it. The Hindu belief in reincarnation has the effect of denying all of our excuses for forgetting our original union with Brahman, claiming that our ignorance is only the karmic result of prior actions. We not only should know better, we can know better through sufficient yogic discipline.

In sum, whether awakened or converted, the conviction of believers is that they have been brought to *the end of their ignorance.* This is a decisive mistake. There is no question that there is not some genuine knowledge, and often a great deal, in every expression of belief. But by confusing belief with universal knowledge, believers place themselves in a curious irony: *they claim a certainty that even knowledge itself does not have.*

This is what we see in the story of Galileo. An ironic reversal has taken place. Urban VIII's accusation was that Galileo's knowledge was actually belief, in this case false belief, and that his own belief was a matter of knowledge. Galileo's consternation rose from his perception that the pope's beliefs were fine; it was knowledge that he lacked, and was unable to grasp the difference. While the pope assumed that belief (for him, knowledge) represented the end of ignorance, Galileo saw it as the beginning of ignorance. Galileo was not a convert. The truth was not revealed to him. He came to it after a lifetime of study. He knew, as any critical thinker would, that knowledge is corrigible, and that belief is rarely so. Open to correction himself, he had no inclination and no reason to take an immovable stand. He could not perform a heroic act like Luther's not because of cowardice but because there was nothing to stand on. Belief systems are already complete. No new knowledge can reverse their finality. Knowledge, in other words, is never knowledge *against*. Galileo knew as well as anyone that there is no protecting ourselves from what discoveries the future brings. In the purest sense, knowers have no personal investment in the truth of their claims, while believers are ready to defend the truth of theirs, sometimes at a high cost. For knowers it is meaningless to die for a mathematical computation that others are bound to discover at another place and time. The test is rudimentary: if I am a knower, I am open to correction; if I am a believer, I resist it. The one says, This is what I am thinking; I will wait for your response to see if it is the truth. The other says, This is what I think; I will wait for you to see it as the truth.

The second response to the objection that we did not desultorily drift into a new belief system, but were converted to it, is that *for this very reason* every act of belief contains the seeds of its own undoing. Its undoing has a double focus: on what comes before belief and what comes afterward, its cause and its consequences.

As for what comes *before*, it is self-evident that, because we cannot know in advance what we will be awakened to believe, we have no control over the source of that belief, whether the source is known or unknown. Note that believing makes sense only if the believer has *not created the object of belief*. Moses did not know in advance what would happen on Mount Sinai. If he had gone there for the purpose of getting his own law approved by God, we would not call it an act of belief, for he would have known exactly what he wanted and how to get a divine imprimatur for what he had already composed. However, he was called by God to receive the law; not any law, but that law in particular. This being the case, what is to prevent God from calling Moses to another law, possibly abnegating the first? In other words, there is no way of being sure we will not be converted again, and again. It has happened often enough. Augustine was converted from his youthful materialism to the strictly moral and dualistic Manicheanism. It was not long before Neoplatonism with its hints of mysticism claimed him as a believer. Only years later was he called to Christianity. This brings us to a particularly rich contradiction built deeply into the phenomenon of belief. Because we cannot get to the object of belief on our own, because the content of our belief has been decided before it has been revealed to us, *belief must carry at its core an element of the unknown*. Contrary to the avowed experience of believers, they have in fact imported an ineradicable uncertainty into their beliefs. They may not be aware of this, or, more likely, they have willfully chosen to ignore it.

The entrance of the unknown applies widely to other religions, as well as to ideological or secular systems of belief. When Moses received the law, it was in two forms, written and oral. Since the oral law can never be accurately captured in words, interpreting it will always be an unfinished task. The law in this case explicitly defies any final reading and its future uses remain unknown. In Hindu scriptures, Krishna was notorious for appearing in unpredictable forms and for being utterly unreliable. In Buddhism, essentially a religion without a deity, there is no guarantee that striving will overcome our suffering. If it does, it comes in a way we could not have foreseen. Even Einstein's sudden insight that mass is relative to velocity, unforeseen by him or anyone else, has become the foundation of vast libraries of solid thinking. But it reminds us that at any point, another insight, also unforeseen, could undo it all. Consider what Einstein did to Newton's tidy universe. Science, at its very best, as in each of these cases, calls for enlightened ignorance.

Therefore, every belief, however passionately held, has a distortion in it. How broad that distortion is, what is concealed by it, how a glance beyond it would change our understanding of the world and our place in it—these are questions that must remain questions. There will always be something the believer does not and cannot know. But this is equally true of knowledge. However carefully knowledge is cleansed of belief, it too carries the unknown within itself. There is no saying what lies beyond its outer limits. How right or wrong it may be, how extensive the void in it, cannot be resolved—ever. *Therefore*, belief is not privileged over knowledge; in spite of the claims of believers, it is fully as open, unfinished, and tentative.

By stressing the matter of unknowability in belief in all its secular as well as religious forms, I want to make it clear that this is not an indirect way of penciling God back into the picture— as some would have it, such as saying that since the world is the way it is, there must be something or *someone* who made it that way. The unknowability stressed here remains unknowability. It is the very essence of higher ignorance. Critics of religion often focus on the attempt to "sneak" God into the picture through a profession of mystery. They are not completely wrong. There are two classic arguments by which believers might indeed make such an attempt. The *cosmological* proof of the existence of God rests on the fact that we have no explanation for the creation of the world; the world, after all, cannot bring itself into existence, even by way of a Big Bang. The *teleological* argument is that the world could not have organized itself as it is; it must therefore have a designer. Critics can easily dispatch these two so-called proofs—often employing strategies from the religions themselves. What is left out of the debate, by both sides, is that the unknown is not only "out there," but also, as Augustine sagely observed, within the self. Unable to scratch away the inconvenient fact that we are at best only partial knowers of ourselves, we may overlook the fact that every personal endeavor carries something unintelligible at its core—including any argument for or against God.

When we consider what comes *after* the passage from unbelief to belief, the issue is nicely captured in a remark by the theologian Tom Driver: "God gave Adam breath, but it was Adam who had to do the breathing." Notice that Adam's creation precedes his breathing. (Breath here is, of course, a metaphor for life.) The sequence is important. However affecting the new insight or the awakening, it *has to find a willing audience*. Paul did not actively conjure up his vision of the crucified Christ, but he went to extraordinary lengths to transform his life to accord with it. In fact, his letters are full of injunctions and suggestions to his readers to live by this same revelation. Obviously, the revelation by itself was not enough. It was only the beginning. In Christian thought the doctrine of grace, or the belief that all things begin with God, including one's salvation, was heavily emphasized by the Protestant reformers of the sixteenth century and their successors.

Where does this appear more clearly than in the sermons of Jonathan Edwards in eighteenth-century New England? In 1742, at the invitation of the pastor of the church in Enfield, Connecticut, Edwards traveled from Northampton, Massachusetts, to deliver what may be the most memorable, certainly the most anthologized, sermon ever to have been heard from an American pulpit, "Sinners in the Hands of an Angry God." The contradiction in question is evident throughout the text. Edwards fervently reminds the congregation that all power lies in the will of the divine, and none in our own. God will both damn and save whom he wishes. "We find it easy to tread on and crush a worm that we see crawling on the earth; so 'tis easy for us to cut or singe a slender thread that anything hangs by; thus easy is it for God when he pleases to cast his enemies down to hell." This we can never know in advance. Still, we can act to avoid it. "Let everyone fly out of Sodom," he urges. In another of his often-cited sermons, he warns listeners not to be satisfied with any knowledge that comes their way, even if it is from the preaching of the word. "But let it be very much your business to search for it, and that with the same diligence and labor with which men are wont to dig in mines of silver and gold."²⁵ On the one hand, damnation and salvation are entirely in the hands of God. On the other, they are entirely in our own. Salvation may come from God, but it must also be received, and vigorously. We might be chosen but we also *choose to be chosen*. And not choose it once, but over and over.

The example is a Christian one, but it applies equally elsewhere. The Buddha, whose crowning insight was that suffering comes from striving, declares to his disciples that they must in effect strive to cease striving. Moses was given the law by Yahweh, but after all it was a *law*, implying that we are as free to obey as not to obey; Yahweh cannot do our obeying for us. Beliefs are not imposed on us; they are not mechanical operations of the gods or of ideologues. Hitler's rousing speeches did not *force* his countrymen to join the National Socialist Party. We are not *compelled* to be socialists or pacifists or creationists. Quite plainly, we can take our beliefs wherever we wish. What could stop us? Only a commitment to the new belief system. Therefore, we find ourselves in Luther's dilemma. Having taken his brave stand before the emperor, he found himself throwing ink at the devil—in fact, fighting with himself to hold on to that "stance." For that reason, every act of belief contains a quarrel with ourselves. To believe is to win an internal struggle—*but one that we have created.*

The conclusion can only be that belief is a thoroughly voluntary act. It may well be initiated by an unsuspected source, but after that it is the believer's project. That introduces another dynamic into our reflection on belief: *morality*. Because we choose what we believe and what we do, we have reasons for our actions, we employ principles of judgment, we subscribe to distinctive sets of values—even though we may seem to be doing only what is "necessary" or "required under the circumstances." Prior to the act, we have already decided what is necessary or required. Believing, strange as it may seem, is therefore a thoroughly moral activity, and our beliefs may be—indeed must be—judged not just for their truthfulness or intelligence but also for where they stand on the continuum between good and evil. Beliefs are not without consequence; they are not "just in our heads." They lead to actions that can have significant results for ourselves and the world around us. Not seeing their voluntary nature is, as noted, an opening to dangerous behavior.

The morality of belief highlights another and very important feature of belief systems. So long as we are acting within a unified and rational network of beliefs, our morality seems to be already decided for us. If we truly believe that the world was created according to the "intelligent" design of a superior, if mysterious, agent, then a number of moral constraints follow. It is a serious offense to our children to allow them to be taught by those who do not have such beliefs. Universities should be required to sponsor debates or colloquia that allow properly believing scientists to confront those who make an academic case for Darwinian evolution. In other words, the rationality and the comprehensiveness of belief systems leave small space for moral indecision or even reflection. In fact, the assumption of the believer is that since it is the system that is the source of morality, dutiful adherence to the prescribed beliefs is therefore inherently moral. One's morality, in this case, is measured by the degree of one's obedience. Properly speaking, it is not the believer who is moral, but the belief system.

The risk is always that believers may consider themselves excused from any higher moral judgment. It is entirely possible, perhaps even common, that faultlessly moral conduct can, from an elevated vantage, seem to be profoundly immoral. This comes from the fact that as faithful members of a particular bounded association of like believers, they are also responsible for the actions of their community as it relates to other communities. Good people can be sponsors of immoral, if not evil, actions on the part of the larger association by which they identify themselves. "My country right or wrong" is a typical cry of moral absolutists. Unfortunately the country may be, and often is, wrong—and its obedient citizens are likely to know it to some degree. This is the famous issue of the collective guilt of German citizens for the crimes of their government in the Hitler years. It has been sufficiently established that if they did not know everything that was happening, they knew enough to be convinced that dreadful crimes were being committed in their names. It is true that the penalty for resisting those actions was high. Still, a decision lay before them: to die or not to die in the defense of a higher morality. It was always possible, of course, to focus on the smaller circles of their collective lives: family, friends, neighbors, jobs. A moral life within this range was attainable. But that did not exempt them from responsibility for the actions of their nation. To use the simplest example, a rail employee could be faithful in seeing that the trains ran on time, but only by ignoring what was being transported. A more complicated example is the mother who is told that if she continues to speak with her Jewish neighbors, they will place her children in an institution.

To be sure, there are some believers who, knowing all this, continue to believe. They understand their belief not as a certainty, but a risk. For all that was said of Paul being a thoroughly persuaded believer, even he betrays a keen sense of risk, especially in his bracing and paradoxical understanding of divine mystery. On the one hand, he can declare, "I am certain nothing will separate me from the love of God in Christ Jesus." He can also say, as in what may be one of his most quoted remarks, "Now we see in a glass darkly, then face to face." The "glass," or "mirror," he refers to is not the clear reflecting surface we are familiar with, but crudely polished metal that shows only the vaguest forms with no identifying detail. We can see "only in part." It is with this thought that many believers would call up Kierkegaard's famous phrase, the "leap of faith," pictured perhaps as a leap from *here* to *there*, leaving out the in-between. "Sure, I can't exactly see what's there," a believer might say, "but I know God would have provided just the right thing." What is usually overlooked, however, is that Kierkegaard said nothing about a safe landing; there was only the leap, and no guarantee of solid ground beyond it. The in-between, or the unknowing, that separates the mirror from what we will see face to face is a true unknowing. The believer, he said, is like a swimmer in a shoreless sea seventy thousand fathoms deep. When that belief has to do with the very meaning of our lives, then that meaning itself is under question.

Some who call themselves believers will say, "Yes, *this* is how I describe the way I believe. My faith has uncertainty, even outright doubt, woven into it. *Nevertheless,* I embrace the risk of a leap into the unseen." I want to emphasize here that this kind of belief, with an acknowledged unknown at its heart, is not the kind that has led to the Age of Faith II with its absolutisms, its certainties, its martyrdoms, and its inevitable drift into violence and warfare. The two kinds must be clearly distinguished. Each represents a corresponding kind of ignorance: for the absolutist believer it is *willful* ignorance, for the believer of the "nevertheless" it is a *learned,* or higher, ignorance.

The line between knowledge and belief is, of course, vulnerable to sudden shifts. On the slightest provocation, the knower can slip over into the category of believer. Anyone remotely familiar with the academic community—which proudly declares itself a sanctuary for the unrestricted pursuit of knowledge—will note how frequently university departments divide into bitter factions. Schools of thought characteristically feed on rivalry with opposing schools, quite as the belief systems that they are. Certain modes of analysis—deconstruction, string theory, feminism, positivism, Marxism, originalism, New Criticism, queer theory—assume the status of dogma. Nonetheless, genuine knowers, uninfected by the spirit of opposition, will eagerly accept the emendation and enlargement of their knowledge from any source, even if the process involves a clamorous exchange of incompatible views.

One easily gets the impression that, overall, believers far outnumber knowers. That may or may not be true, but what can be seen is that knowledge has little influence over belief. Two political parties, for example, can be in such dispute with each other that no amount of knowledge will modify their beliefs. Those who believe that global warming is well under way have amassed a mountain of supporting data; disbelievers have their own data; each accuses the other of ideological distortion. Will more knowledge resolve the issue? It may, but not soon.

Generally, knowers have no need to win over resistant believers. Their only need is to enter into dialogue with others committed to the labor of extending the field of knowledge. Research scientists (knowers) working in the field of evolutionary theory have little interest in contesting the claims of the advocates of "intelligent design" (believers). The growing body of champions for intelligent design, on the other hand, have aggressively attacked the scientists for their errors, the result of their belief in a godless and mechanical universe,[26] shades of Galileo and the pope.

There are instances, to be sure, where certain beliefs are so dangerous or abhorrent that knowledge is called to the task of defanging them. Theories of racial supremacy, exploitation of the world's finite physical resources, the cleansing of national memories of past atrocities, wildly false speculations on the origin of AIDS, the claimed superiority of a certain form of government or a certain national culture—these belong to a long list of beliefs that can and have had disastrous results. Still, knowledge as a disabling strategy has few clear victories. Again and again, beliefs stand firm against charges of misinformation, distortion, and inanity.

Knowing and believing are so different that they seem to represent two ways of being in the world, one unfinished and open, the other fixed and defiant. It is as if the mirror that believers gaze into reproduces precisely what is there, and the mirror that knowers hold up to the world and themselves has a scored and distorting surface.

To summarize, there is a substantial objection to the presentation of belief made in this book. It is that for most believers, the experience of coming to believe is that of being *called*, or *chosen*, or *being confronted*. It is as though it has come to me from without, an origin anywhere but in myself. Because of this, a clear line has been crossed; on one side what has been rejected, on the other the truth. Crossing the line is not therefore a gradual process. Becoming a believer is undergoing a conversion, or a turning around and going in the opposite direction. For the most part, the beliefs left behind and those gained are mirror images of each other. Such a conversion comes with certainty, a conviction we have moved into a realm of solid knowledge— even if we have not yet grasped it all. This has a strange consequence, unacknowledged by the believer: belief takes on a certainty that knowledge itself does not have—the error made by Galileo's inquisitors. In fact, knowledge is infinitely corrigible; unlike belief, it can be altered or canceled by new information. Belief, in other words, is a corrupted form of knowledge—one that refuses correction. There are two responses to this view of belief, based on what comes *before* its acquisition and what comes *after*. (1) Because we are chosen to believe by something outside ourselves, we took no role in the act. The very act of belief, in that case, contains within itself an unknown that restores the uncertainty believers thought they had surpassed. (2) Once chosen, believers must still choose to accept what is offered, or choose to be chosen. This gives belief a voluntary nature that puts the believer under moral judgment for choosing that set of beliefs. Belief therefore has a tenacity that defies both intellectual and moral correction.

These remarks have led to something of a conundrum. If both the *before* and the *after* of an awakening leave us without any limit to which the voluntary act of belief can take us, does it not follow that there are no criteria of judgment as to what is true or false? Have we slid into self-defeating relativism where everything has the same value—a sure path to nihilism? The answer is no, there are limits, but how these limits are understood and applied requires more reflection.

As we have turned to Luther for a useful definition of belief, and to Galileo for a distinction between belief and knowledge, we call up another historical figure, one renowned for his attention to clarifying boundaries and building structures to protect them. When Hadrian erected his wall across the neck of England, a prodigious four-year project completed in 126 CE, it was not because he had an aesthetic interest in stonework. Across that wall were fierce tribes capable of doing great damage to the territory that Rome had civilized. The Romans did not civilize indifferently. With centuries of practice, they knew to support enough of the local customs to keep relative peace among the conquered. Commerce was encouraged by the building of roads and market centers. Grand theaters where the performance of drama was accompanied by elaborate technological innovations were but part of the artistic life that flourished under their control. Hadrian, himself gifted in music and the arts, devoted considerable energy to this end. Schools were established, artisans were professionally trained, champion athletes were celebrated. Latin was taught as both the official and cultural language. The law was severely enforced but it was uniform, comprehensive, and just. There was, in brief, much to lose should the invading hordes sweep down from the north.

The wall served Hadrian and the Romans not just to hold off fierce and uncivilized attackers. Like other boundaries of the empire, it also defined what was contained. Rome on one side, danger and chaos on the other. To be a Roman was to know exactly what your place was in the official order, whether it was slave or aedile, senator or legionnaire. Citizenship itself was protected by the clear limits of the boundary. Any breaching of the protective wall, therefore, was sure to bring more than physical destruction. One's very identity as a Roman was at stake; so too were all the familiar, if worn, paths of acceptable social behavior. One's property, family, military or political titles, modes of commerce, plans for the future of one's children, choice of neighbors—all this depended on the rigid, plainly demarcated, heavily defended frontiers of empire. All the lines one draws within society, even within oneself, depend on these unbreachable limits. It is no surprise that Terminus, the Roman god of boundaries, is unaffected by efforts to dislodge him from where he has settled, even when the efforts are of the other gods. He was right to do so, to a point.

As indicated, a belief system is effective only if it can place itself in opposition to another, and the more threatening the opposition the better. Here, too, without an enemy the wall becomes meaningless, no more than mere entertainment, a decorative piece of masonry. Decoration (the arts in general) is no protection against foreign elements, not only in the streets of the citizenry but in their minds as well. Certainly aware of this, the Romans found it necessary not only to shield themselves but to *provoke alien forces* from which protection was necessary. Roman society absolutely depended on whatever opposed it. The definition of what it meant to be a Roman only made sense against the barbarians. There was no alternative. One was a Roman or a barbarian. The very word "barbarian" comes from the strange sounds of foreign speech that to the Roman ear sounded like meaningless syllables: bar-bar-bar (blah-blah-blah?). Therefore, without barbarians, even language opens itself to a new and confounding vocabulary. We need a clear grasp of what is nonsense merely to make sense.

Boundaries are also within oneself. The danger of breaches in the outer walls of empire is accompanied by the danger that internalized boundaries could give way. There is always a risk that a Roman can loosen the inner structure of citizenship and convert to political and cultural barbarism. The effectiveness of inner restraints has the same dynamic as the outer: to be a boundary at all it requires an opposing force—in this case, within the self. Each Roman—each member of an ordered society—must live with this inner conflict. To *be* a Roman, it is necessary to possess threatening barbarian impulses requiring constant vigilance. Without them, conventions of acceptable behavior lose their appeal. To the church, Luther was a barbarian; and, as we saw, he was a barbarian to himself, struggling with the demonic forces of his own doubt. The inner boundaries and the outer must function in tandem, strengthening each other. Neither can exist without the other.

Gathering at every corner of a belief system are the equivalent of Picts, Gaels, Carthaginians, Celts, Franks, Gauls, Scythians, Teutons, Huns, Vandals, Parthians, Goths (or what we might call Islamists, Christian fundamentalists, and "secular humanists") without and within, all eager to trash everything that we consider precious, all that we have accumulated by long and patient labor. Our very identity as believers is at stake. Once these pagan attackers break into the kingdom, there is no saying what we may be forced to do. Could we be forbidden to worship in the familiar way, required to add new divinities, obey arbitrary and cruel laws, speak profane languages, and answer to charges of falsehood and treachery? Much worse, might we be seduced into a new way of thinking?

What Hadrian wanted was a *civitas*, a society ruled by law and so structured that citizens knew where they belonged, where the limits of social and personal behavior were clear and unchanging. The reach of the emperor's authority was deep, shaping all the basic institutions of society—the family, the military, slavery, taxation, the minting of coins, education, temple worship, commerce, the practice of law, prostitution, entertainment, the punishment of criminals and enemies. It was not so rigid that there was no social mobility, but any extreme deviations were carefully monitored. The Roman *civitas,* though often ruled by elected officials, was governed from the top down. Ethnicity and class were closely defined and beyond challenge. (Hadrian himself, though of sufficient nobility to serve as emperor, was sometimes mocked for his Spanish origin and accent.)

Although the reach of authority in the Roman *civitas* was deep, it was remarkably stable. Change was rare. Rules of behavior were clear and predictable. To the good fortune of the Roman Britons, however, Hadrian was mistaken in what he thought the wall would do. Determined to make it effective, he went so far as to carve lines in the whitewashed exterior to make it more visually brilliant and thus all the more obvious to the barbarians. However, only a few years elapsed before an active trade developed with the northern tribes. It is true, they never converted to Roman citizenship, but because of their differences both sides profited from it. A good bit of hostility remained. The wall was occasionally breached and rebuilt, but for long periods it was simply ignored. A curious oversight on Hadrian's part was that while he kept the northern tribes out, he kept a good dozen other tribes *within* the wall, some of them fiercely independent of Rome. The result was a social and economic vitality that made Britain for several centuries one of the most prosperous and peaceful of Roman territories. Most of the problems in governing came in fact not from the Britons but from devious and often murderous politics in Rome itself.

It is true that boundaries can serve to prevent descending into chaos. However, for the boundaries to have functioned for the citizens as Hadrian intended would have had a suffocating effect on the society: it would become repetitious and dispirited, its internal conflicts poisonous, its unity fractured by self-interest. The *civitas* functioned best when its imperfections were sufficient to allow citizens greater flexibility in the shaping of their lives.

It is worth noting that in considering Hadrian as an illustration of a believer's use of boundaries, there comes into view yet another feature of belief. Note that it was as a *military* figure that he built and defended the walls. This fact exposes the close association of belief and war. Believers and warriors tend to merge into one another: the military sees itself in religious terms, while believers take on the images of warfare. Armies are sent on *missions* to bring *peace* and *freedom* to the world. Major encounters are known as *crusades*. Soldiers are subjected to transforming *initiations* in which they become not only "real" men but *new beings*. They are admitted into an exclusive *brotherhood*, with a *monastic* discipline, and like monks are pledged to *poverty* and are essentially *celibate*. They are fitted into a *hierarchy* (Gr.: priestly rule) to which they are *faithfully obedient*. They speak of being *baptized by fire*, and of *making the ultimate sacrifice*. Giving their lives to *save others from harm* is especially praised. *Suffering* and *self-abasement* are regular features of their personal lives. Monuments to their victories resemble *temples*. Military heroes are celebrated by bronze and marble statues that could serve for the *Olympian deities*. They are attended by *priests* who serve them *sacraments*, *hear their confessions*, and encourage them to return to battle. Soldiers are *robed*, or uniformed, as priests themselves, in identical clothing that sets them off from the unbaptized. The uniformity goes deeper; they are *one with the body* of their sacred society, and have no identity beyond it. They are *ordained* to their rank and order, known chiefly by the number they wear around their necks like a *holy amulet*. The world they are *chosen* to protect is surrounded by deadly enemies. There is a complete division of *good and evil*. They speak of *triumph* and of *ultimate victory*. The *purple heart* is a common icon in Christian churches, referring to the wounds sustained by Jesus.

Just as they think of themselves in religious terms, believers freely adopt military imagery. They speak of being the *army of God*, *Christian soldiers*; the Crusaders were known as *knights of Christ*, having formally chosen to *"take the cross,"* which they then sewed on their tunics and wore into battle. Luther's great hymn calls God *a mighty fortress*. A popular nineteenth-century hymn begins, *Onward Christian soldiers*. They engage in *moral crusades* and conduct *campaigns* for functions as varied as fund-raising and electing Christians to public office. Muslims speak of the advance of faith as *jihad*. The national flag—a universal symbol of warfare—hangs in American churches. The swastika was prominent in German churches during that notorious decade. Taking a treasured place in Hindu scriptures is the *Mahabharata*, possibly the longest poem ever written, which is essentially the story of a vast war—during which the god Krishna tells Prince Arjuna it is his *religious duty to enter the battle*, even though he has relatives on both sides. It is often pointed out that Jesus apparently permitted Peter, his closest disciple, to carry a *sword*, and said nothing when Peter used it. Christian believers speak of

Armageddon, the cosmic *battle* that coincides with the second coming of Jesus. In popular literature, Jesus is portrayed as a brilliant and ruthless *general* in this final war. Mao's Long March has become a popular *pilgrimage*. Bodhisattvas are often represented in Buddhist temples as *ferocious warriors*. The memorial in Washington for Abraham Lincoln, America's greatest war president at the time of its greatest war, presents him as a god in his temple, towering over the worshiping mortals at the feet of his throne. Some American Christians (self-identified "fundamentalists") have taken as their hero not Lincoln, but General Stonewall Jackson, a brilliant but savage military leader, for his deep and oft-avowed faith. His recommendation to fellow believers was to *"draw the sword and throw away the sheaf."*

But the overlap is more than metaphorical. Constantine declared by royal fiat that Christianity was to be the official religion of the Roman Empire. Popes fielded armies. A succession of Holy Roman Emperors ruled and protected the church by military and political might. The English monarchy is known officially as Defender of the Faith. Christianity is the state church in a number of European countries. Muhammad's initial fame was as a general, leading an army to liberate Mecca from infidels. An increasing number of Muslims are dreaming of restoring the caliphate, or empire, that was formed during the first Islamic century. Kamikaze pilots acted out of religious devotion. Suicide bombers justify their actions as acts of faith, earning them the status of martyr. Warriors everywhere are sent to create and defend a sacred *realm*; believers everywhere work to bring in the *kingdom of God*, to establish a divine *reign* on earth.

. . .

To use the appropriate metaphor, we can say that the Britons kept their eye both on the *boundaries* of their society and on the *horizon* of that which lay beyond it. Boundary and horizon are not incompatible but they have very different characteristics. Unlike a boundary, a horizon does not have a fixed outer edge. It is not a line drawn by someone else, but the limit of one's own vision. If we walk to the point where our vision was thought to end, the horizon will only have extended itself. Everything within a boundary has its identity, its definition, its proper place only because there are immovable limits. Nothing within a horizon can have a fixed definition. Every step taken alters the horizon, changes the field of vision, causing us to see what had been thus far circumscribed as something quite different. To the child, a parent will be understood entirely within a predictable role. To the adult, the parent wears a very different aspect. The parent is the same person, but now seen in a way unimaginable to the child.

Because horizon is the end of vision, and because every move we make gives the field an aspect we couldn't have noticed before, what lies beyond the horizon cannot be known. (Otherwise it would be within the horizon.) As with the angelic messenger, there is no control over what comes into our vision. We know only that if we shift our location, something new will come into view. So to shift is indeed to risk, or leap. And not everything that results is either desired or desirable. There are experiences and new information that will show the familiar as strange, the comforting as dangerous, the adjacent as distant. It can disturb as well as edify. Moreover, not every shift of the viewer will reveal something significant. It can be just more of the same, or nothing worth reflecting on. And yet without that shift, we begin to lose our vision altogether: what is seen over and over again ceases to be seen. What doesn't appear in a fresh way will be thought changeless and ordinary, no longer a stimulus to thought. Learning is reduced to mere repetition and can only confirm what has already been known. Friendships become static, empty of expectations for the future. The outcome of all our efforts becomes predictable. All mysteries can be explained. All dimensions and measurements hold. To be aware of our horizons is to live in wonder.

To use another metaphor, boundaries necessary to life are like a protective film or skin without which the organism would quickly perish. But if the skin were impermeable it would perish just as certainly. The body can survive only by an ongoing and dynamic relation with the surrounding world, some of which is injurious and some essential to health. Some, though not all, of what the barbarians provide is bracing and awakening, while some of what the caesars provide is viral and cancerous. There is, in fact, a great deal of commerce of this kind. An immeasurably broad range of nourishing and supporting and harmful materials are in constant exchange. The marvel is that within a vigorous dynamic, however great the changes we pass through, the identity of the self need not be lost.

There is no better example of the effective balance between boundary and horizon than in the multiplication of creeds in Christian history. The point of a creed is to protect what lies inside the acceptable realm of belief from the unacceptable without. It is a kind of gatekeeper, determining what should be included and what should be rejected. The first creeds appear in rudimentary form in the New Testament. In the gospel of Mark, Jesus was asked, "Which commandment is the first of all?" He answers in the words of the Jewish Shema, itself a kind of creed: "The first is, 'Hear, O Israel: the Lord our God, the Lord is one; and you shall love the Lord your God with all your heart, and with all your soul, and with all your mind, and with all your strength.'" This quickly proves far too vague for the developing Christian church, concerned to keep a clear definition of heresy (from the Greek for "other"). A classic refinement, the Apostles' Creed, written sometime in the second century, has long been a staple of Christian confession. But it too has dangerous gaps open to false believers. Another Roman emperor, Constantine, two hundred years after Hadrian, built a wall of another kind. A recent convert, disturbed by divisions within Christendom (and in the empire), he convened a synod of bishops in the year 325, in the small town of Nicaea across the Bosporus from the recently renamed city of Constantinople. The resulting Nicene Creed set a standard for distinguishing orthodoxy from heterodoxy that holds its authority to this day. But neither of these creeds, nor the words of Jesus himself, were sufficient. Over the centuries, as mentioned, *hundreds* of creeds,[27] *thousands* of papal bulls, countless official resolutions, and binding councils have been required to keep the wall intact. But obviously, from the very fact of their endless reproduction, not one of them has completely succeeded. On the whole, however, they have succeeded, if unintentionally, in admitting just enough variant thinking that the faith has maintained its remarkable vitality—without losing its identity. Christianity's good fortune is the inefficiency of its gatekeepers.

The obvious lesson is that when belief goes back and forth on the same familiar paths, it loses sight of the unexplored regions just beyond its gaze, and begins to think that what is familiar is all there is. True belief is a matter of walking marked paths with muscular self-control, along tracks worn bare by preceding generations of marchers. It is in this respect that expanding horizons, the gifts of original if not irreverent visionaries to every belief system, have a protective function. What officialdom dreads is also a source of its evolving vitality.

Yet if belief were entirely horizonal it would become a wash of weightless and inconsequent ideas. Just as if it were entirely bounded it would become mindless chatter. The task is to find just the right way of blending what is certain with the uncertain, the known with what is unknown: neither knowledge without wonder nor belief without horizon.

The operative principle here is that if vision is restricted to a belief system, or if it is divorced from all belief systems, it ceases to be vision. What is necessary is that it not restrict itself to a belief system but that belief systems always fall within the scope of poetic horizons. For this reason, horizons and belief systems are not opposites. They occur simultaneously. Many belief systems may come into view within the scope of a horizon, including one's own. Visionaries (what we shall refer to as poets) do not destroy the walls, but show the openings through them. They do not promise what believers will see, only that the walls do not contain the horizon.

. . .

Here we meet a nettlesome terminological confusion. I have used a multiplicity of words as synonyms for religion: association, institution, practice, tradition, people, body, community. Each word has its own limitations, chiefly because it does not point us to the uniqueness of a religion's identity. To call a particular religion a community suggests that it is *one of* any number of communities. As an institution, it can be confused with political entities, cultural movements, and assorted collective enterprises. We cannot say exactly what a religion *is*, and yet it plainly involves an impact on the world by a unified collective. It is for this reason that I employ the term *communitas*. As previously indicated, Hadrian's driving goal was to establish and maintain the Roman *civitas*. The term is not to be confused with *communitas*. The difference between them? One is dependent on rulers to protect its integrity and authorities to guide its beliefs; the other is a spontaneous gathering of persons who identify themselves and one another as members of a unified body. The two are quite distinct but they are also companions. *Communitas* cannot be created. It evolves spontaneously out of the desire of its participants to get to the bottom of the very mystery that brings them together. It matters little where that desire is directed—to the quest for the "real" Jesus, or the final interpretation of the Mosaic law, or the true dharma, or the correct reading of the Quran, or the perfect socialist society. *Civitas* can only be intentionally created from without. It is an artifact of monarchs, or philosophers, or elected parliaments, or revolutionaries. It can exist only within carefully devised boundaries. It functions most successfully when its belief system is both clear and broadly held. *Communitas*, because it is spontaneous, organizes from the bottom up, its structure accidental, its future open, its beliefs unformed. It has no *civitas* of its own, although it will always be found in one *civitas* or another. Because its identity is not established within boundaries, it remains untouched by the surrounding *civitas*. For example, Judaism was a presence in the *civitas* of Rome for all seven of its centuries, and while there were distinct Roman influences on the Jewish tradition, it succeeded in preserving its distinctiveness. When Rome disappeared, the Jewish *communitas* was hardly affected; its members were no less Jewish, nor did they ever think of themselves as Romans. The history of the Christian *communitas* in Rome is more complicated. For two centuries it thrived through episodes of savage persecution. Then Constantine, converted to the faith in the year 312, sought to make the empire Christian. The favor was returned by Christians when they made of themselves an empire, under papal rule. Rome, it seems, was strikingly successful at tempting Christians into belief systems that cohered with its imperial designs. Nonetheless, the genuine Christian *communitas*, though severely diminished and endangered, never compromised its identity. To the present, however, many Christians are still tempted by dreams of social and political rule. It is not unthinkable that in time some of Rome's successors will absorb them all, effectively creating an imperial Christendom, and erasing the historic *communitas*.

Strictly speaking, *communitas* has no plural form. That is to say, there is not one *communitas* here and another there. The reason for this is the inherent compatibility of every expression of *communitas*. Nineteenth-century French artists found Chinese art extraordinary in its use of materials, its novel styles, and the talent of its artists. The influences were strong and immediate. One art expanded the possibilities of another. They were not two bodies of artists resolved to transform the other into copies of themselves. Language, ritual, humor, architecture, philosophy, cuisine, theater, agriculture, couture, music, religion—all are regions in which the lines between one *communitas* and another are easily crossed. There may well be a competitive spirit at work through all of this. One style of theater, one school of philosophy, one form of street talk are often meant to succeed all those before them. However, insofar as they have no intention of silencing others or converting them to their own style, or insofar as they fail to do so, the shared *communitas* has only been enriched. The effects are cumulative. *Communitas* is distinctive in another sense: just as it is not restricted to one group of persons, nor to one geographical location, it is free of temporal exclusion. The Renaissance, after all, was a designed "rebirth" of classical styles dead for centuries. The paintings of Lascaux are as little time-bound as those of Van Gogh. As the philosopher A. N. Whitehead put it, Western thought is but a footnote to Plato; we are still at work on the problems he presented. The *Analects* of Confucius reveal as much about ancient Asian culture as about the present. Nonetheless, there is some awkwardness in the use of the term when speaking of expressions of *communitas* found chiefly in different places and times. For the sake of eliminating annoying verbal twists, and for that sake only, I will occasionally refer to this *communitas* or that one, trusting that the reader understands the inherent, if not apparent, continuity of one expression with all others.

. . .

Lying always in the near background of the discussion of belief is the issue of authority. Like belief, it is a complicated and
nuanced subject, far richer than the popular view that an authority is someone or something that instructs or forces us into a
preshaped agenda of thought and action, leaving us with a choice
either to obey or rebel. As I had made use earlier of Galileo,
Luther, and Hadrian as illustrations of the dynamic of belief,
for an understanding of the issue of authority I turn now to a
well-studied historical event: the Second Inaugural speech of
Abraham Lincoln, a few brief sentences from the steps of the
U.S. Capitol on March 4, 1865. The end of the Civil War with its
horrific losses to both sides was a few months in coming, but it
had recently become clear that victory would go to the Union
forces. As little as nine months earlier, the outcome was still in
doubt and the president was thought so weakened by the progress
of the war that he was unlikely even to win a nomination as candidate for a second term. A sudden reversal in the North's for-
tunes on the battlefield changed everything. The president was
strongly reelected. The public rightly expected a victory speech
celebrating the triumphant end of both election and war. That is
not what they got.[28]

When the hurrahs that accompanied his presentation to the
crowd died away, Lincoln delivered an address of 703 words that
took no more than six or seven minutes to read. It came and
went so quickly that hundreds were rushing to join the enormous audience that was still forming when he had finished. The
words themselves, however, continue to be heard. Lincoln's

Second Inaugural belongs as permanently to the nation's self-understanding as the Constitution itself. It is a work of literature that, though written in simple words, and most of those of one syllable, is so elegantly constructed that no summary can capture its multiple meanings.

Although both the words and their delivery were somber, Lincoln does in fact begin by acknowledging that it is "as well known to the public as to myself" that the North has effectively won the war, thus preserving the Union. That he believes the North has been, from the beginning, morally superior to the forces of the Confederacy is evident in his claim that at the time of the First Inaugural "insurgent agents were in the city seeking to *destroy*" the Union by "negotiation." The implication is that what they could not accomplish by political persuasion they would achieve by war. No one wanted this war, but one party "would rather *make* war rather than let the nation survive; and the other would *accept* war rather than let it perish." This puts the cause of the war clearly in the hands of the "other" party. Lincoln, we understand from this, had no choice but to go to war. Thus the chilling sentence, "And the war came."

So far, the president appears disingenuous. Let us remember that the Civil War was above all a collision of believers. Each side had a coherent and comprehensive view of what was at issue. Strong theories of government, the economy, domestic life, and religion gave measurable weight to their arguments. They had a full complement of heroic narrative, oratorical eloquence, and ceremonial pomp. There was a genuine love of the land, South and North. Lincoln himself went to war for an idea. Many times he referred to the importance of Union, as if it were a divine

mandate. In this respect, Lincoln is a true believer, willing to sacrifice more than half a million young men to protect the idea of
Union. It can, of course, be argued that saving the Union was
worth the sacrifice (especially if you include the end of slavery
as part of it; not everyone did, including Lincoln himself at the
conflict's beginning). But what made it a divine mandate? For
what reason was it necessary to preserve the Union? To this point
in the address, these are the words of an ideologue claiming absolute authority for his actions.

Then, a few sentences later, comes the majestic remark that
gives the address as a whole an altogether different meaning.
Both sides in the war, he said, "read the same Bible, and pray to
the same God; and each invokes His aid against the other. . . . The
prayers of both could not be answered; that of neither has been
answered fully." All claims that anyone, including himself, is acting on a divine mandate are at best an illusion. With these words,
he has placed all ideology, indeed all belief, under the final un-
intelligibility of a God who answers prayers, if at all, as he
wishes, not as we wish. No longer can any one of us claim God
as an authority. Inasmuch as God was generally thought of as
Supreme Authority, Lincoln is declaring by implication that there
is no authority at all to whom we can turn for a final claim to
truth. This Lincoln is no ideologue, not even a true believer; he
is the very portrait of higher ignorance.

These "two Lincolns" are in only apparent contradiction. In
the initial paragraphs, he was speaking as the president-elect, the
chief of state, commander of the armed forces. As such he has
fulfilled his civic responsibilities. He has successfully defended
the *civitas* he was chosen to defend. In that role, it is perhaps ap-

propriate that he cite God's approval for these actions, even if it is a tribal god. But then we learn that it is the "other" Lincoln who is really speaking these words. As a human being, as a person of profound ignorance, he must immediately qualify what he had just said in his theatrical role as protector of the *civitas*. However we might be inclined to present ourselves as the true victors in this war, in fact there are no victors. We are not whom we represent ourselves to be. "And the war came." The irony in this famous sentence is only too obvious. The war did not do its own fighting. It was we who chose to enter it. We preferred war over any other means of reconciling our competing beliefs. Neither party expected that "the *cause* of the conflict might cease with, or even before, the conflict itself should cease." In the end, there is only the war, our war.

It is instructive to compare the Second Inaugural with Lincoln's other great speech. As a work of poetry, the Gettysburg Address far excels this one. It takes its place in world literature alongside the Eighth Psalm and Hamlet's first monologue. It is likely the best-known speech ever delivered. And yet it harbors a danger that the Second Inaugural explicitly avoids. It praises the war dead, it promises never to forget them, and it resolves to complete what was there begun. It is a heroic paean that edges toward the glorification of war. This was an address Lincoln could not have delivered in 1865.

What confronts us in the Second Inaugural is a stark contrast between two kinds of authority. The first kind is perfectly obvious. It is the authority that has its natural home in belief systems, and is necessary to sustain the *civitas*. As such, it is an exercise of power. The second is much less obvious. It is the authority that forms the bonds of *communitas*. It is a work of what, following Plato, we can call poetry. Crudely put, the one is preconceived and imposed, the other spontaneous and expansive. Each requires its analysis.

As made use of by believers, authority, whether it is of a text or a person or an institution or an event, is essentially *restrictive*. Its primary function is to halt the dilution of belief, to block exits into the competing regions of unbelief. It is often assigned imperial status. The proper reaction to it is one of obedience. The boundaries are fixed, inviolable, and permanent; they are not subject to compromise or accommodation. As noted before, believers are free to move as they will within established limits, but never beyond them. Those limits are the final reference for all disputes, the concluding arbiter of differences that occur within the realm of belief. Our labors within that realm have the burden of rendering acceptable thought both rational and plausible—but always in agreement with the designated authority. Antiauthoritarianism is therefore the gravest danger within any given belief system.

Authority as power, of course, works in both directions. If it is restrictive it is also *protective*. It functions as a kind of carapace, restricting movement but also protecting against injury. Believers are not only required to stay within their boundaries, they are free to move around in them only if those boundaries are secure and their community sheltered. In this respect, authority directs its attention to opposing and especially threatening authorities. It has an aggressive, even bellicose function. To be in struggle is essential to its acknowledgment as power. For the gathered crowd, Lincoln was not standing at the podium as a figure of tragic and poetic genius, as we know him to be, but as a conquering chieftain who by awesome force has just driven back an enemy that threatened the boundaries of the state. In the same way, Charles came to Worms not only to define the outer limits of orthodoxy, but to act in the imperial role of directing his forces at a presumed enemy, thus demonstrating to the Holy Roman Empire that he was worthy to be called its protector. The theatrical aspect of the encounter was essential. It was designed to guarantee an applauding audience. The realm had to be aware that it was being protected by the warlike actions of its master.

By pointing to the association of authority with power, I may seem to be suggesting that authoritarian systems are uniformly oppressive. More often a powerful and effective authority is experienced as *comforting*. Believers commonly love their authorities, even when they are severe. It is hardly rare for believers to approve of the sanctions imposed on them, even when they entail extreme punishment. Punishment, too, can be loved and sought after. Self-humiliation among medieval monastics, as an acknowledgment of their sinful rebellion against God, was common and often took exaggerated forms—including such regimens as starvation, sleeping on the stone floors of unheated cells, walling themselves in for a lifetime of isolation. Saint Catherine of Siena once expressed her self-punishment by drinking a container of pus drawn from her ill patients. Victims of Stalin often expressed their love for him as they were led to execution. Islamic fakirs, among other forms of self-humiliation, wore uncomfortable clothes that contained breeding colonies of noxious insects.

Such forms of self-humiliation are especially comforting when they share the dreadful suffering of the authority in question. Shiite Muslims lash themselves with lacerating instruments in memory of the suffering of their martyred founder, Ali. There is a practice among Chinese communists of replicating Mao's famous march with all of its hardship and deprivation. Christians regularly see their misfortune and tragedies as a participation in the suffering of Jesus. I cite these regimens not to show how terrible they are so much as how they express consolation and adoration for the believer's designated authority. There are, of course, countless ways exultant gratitude and praise are expressed: dancing, singing, private and collective prayer, pilgrimages, the building of mosques, temples, and cathedrals on places considered sacred. In all these instances, the *experience* of believers is not one of being under the domination of a brutal and uncaring power.

If restriction, protection, and comfort are proper functions of authority understood as power, so is *authentication*. Perfect agreement with the network of beliefs under protection allows the believer to speak with the voice of the protector and the privilege of restricting. In that sense, authority constantly replicates itself within the community of true believers. Che Guevara had so identified himself with Castro and his ideology that he came to embody the very essence of the revolution, speaking with an authority equal to the premier. Justices of the U.S. Supreme Court have a voice as authentic as that of the Constitution itself.

Closely associated with authentication is the responsibility of authority as *guide*. Although believers are free to wander where they will within their particular orthodoxy, they need help from those who are authenticated as its most faithful interpreters—and are therefore assumed to have a deeper knowledge of the possibilities. The instructional and inspirational task is so important to authoritarian structures that great attention is given to education, often redesigning entire school and university curricula (to deal with the falsehoods in the theory of evolution, say, and correct misconceptions of history) and instituting elaborate programs of instruction and training in the society's most treasured beliefs (the Soviet Pioneers, the Boy Scouts of America, the Harvard Business School). As with authentication, there can be nothing original in the instructing voice. It must faithfully reproduce the prevailing orthodoxy. Essentially it plays the role of broadcaster, announcing to a wider audience the scope of acceptable thinking. A former U.S. department secretary is a welcome member of the Harvard Business School; Venezuela's president, Hugo Chavez, is not. There is concern among American conservatives that universities have declared them enemies to the liberal system of beliefs that is seen to prevail in the academy.

Because we place authority in the role of protecting us, we have an equal obligation to *protect our authorities,* that is, to do all that is necessary to maintain the illusion that we are in their service, and not they in ours. Whether it is presumed to originate entirely in a single person (emperor, president, pope), an institution (comintern, parliament, synod), or a text (Quran, the U.S. Constitution, the Code of Hammurabi, Mao's Little Red Book), the obligation applies. The sacred text may not be defiled, but must be treated with ceremonial respect. The Torah is securely contained in the Torah ark, and when presented to the congregation is met with elaborate ritualized reverence. The Bible commonly has its own elevated pulpit in Christian churches. The pope is surrounded by Swiss guards, the king by his court, the president by Secret Service agents. A rich array of behavioral gestures exists to display the obeisance of believers to their authority: kissing the ring, kneeling, using honorific names and titles, bowing, saluting, hurrahing, applauding, lowering one's head, removing one's hat, lying prone, looking in another direction, using a specialized vocabulary, limiting one's speech to certain topics. Acts of extreme sacrifice and self-denial are often appropriate: risking one's life to defend the king, or the flag, or the nation, or the Quran. All such acts are intended to magnify the power of authority, not only over nonbelievers, but also over themselves.

In spite of the profound respect offered the sources of authority, it is still the case that belief cannot be *imposed*. If we were forced to believe, it would not be belief but a mere mechanical iteration. Even under threat of extreme punishment, we can at best mouth the prescribed phrases. For this reason, when authority is ignored, it has no means of remaining a true authority. Pronouncements from Soviet rulers, for example, were increasingly shrugged off by their subjects as irrelevant or even absurd. Losing the supporting fervor of believers, they could control their population only by threats of severe military and judicial action. Although these powers were pervasive and enormously feared, the nation became a soulless shell. The citizenry learned to speak the language of Marxism quite without the least belief in its truths. Official statements were regarded as little more than intrusive noise. The Soviet rulers confused authority with power, failing to understand that power by itself has no authority, and authority has only the power its observers give it. Collapse was inevitable.

However committed believers, and citizens, are to their authorities, there is a withering irony in their use of it. *Authority does not precede its use, but is created by it.* It does not present itself spontaneously; it is *chosen* by those whom it restricts, protects, authenticates, and guides. There is a reflexive action in the creation of authority that echoes the contradictory nature of belief as we have discussed it. Sacred scriptures are not sacred merely because they are printed on the page; they are thought to be so only when their readers elevate them to that status. A teacher to whom no students come, a physician without patients, a bible that no one reads, a god whom no one worships, a preacher without a church, a king whom no one obeys may intend to play those roles, but without appropriate response they are unworthy of the name. In most religions and spiritual traditions, gurus, swamis, ayatollahs, healers, seers, saints, prophets, shamans, sages, avatars, visionaries, spirit guides are designated by those who come to them. Merely to make an announcement that one has assumed any of these functions is not enough; neither does elaborate training automatically confer authority. The Buddha, when asked to name a successor, responded by surrendering himself to whatever use they would make of his teachings, transferring authority from himself to his followers. The Dalai Lama does not announce himself but must be found by an arduous search, as if it is the searchers and not the sought who determine his identity. Contrary to the popular notion, authority does not come from the top down but from the bottom up.

Authority understood as power, in other words, repeats the contradictions we saw in belief as such. Its restrictive function is an act of self-restriction, as it is in its other functions. In an ironic twist, it is not the authority that instructs us, but we who instruct the authority; it is not the authority that has taken on imperial powers, it is we who have named the emperor. The Constitution does not tell us what to make of it; we first make of it what we wish, and then falsely claim its authority as the source of our beliefs. We do not go to an authority to learn how to act, what to study, what to say. We *decide beforehand* what we expect it to provide. Effective authorities are thoroughly obedient.

There is another use of authority, entirely different from the first. We see it in the familiar practice of "consulting an authority," understood as an open-minded inquiry. Approaching authority in this latter way implies that we go there to learn something so far hidden from us. Not only do we not know what we will find, we cannot be sure we will find anything, or whether what we find will be unsettling or alarming. There is even some guesswork involved as to locating an appropriate source. To whom do we turn to learn the causes of mental illness or the outcome of a war? Psychoanalysts, astrologers, neurologists, oracles, political theorists, our own experience? What is more, and most important, authority of this latter kind can appear without our inquiring, bringing news we did not know we needed.

The clue to understanding this second use of authority lies in the background of the Latin word for authority: *auctoritas*, from the word *auctor*, or author. The *auctor* is not just a producer of literature, but an inventor or creator of new thoughts and ideas. Reaching back into etymological history, *auctores* are messengers from another region, one so far unknown to us. They can be the source of surprising information, sometimes of great importance to our lives, sometimes merely amusing or too enigmatic to be useful. Whether these revelations derive from the *auctor's* direct experience or from the imagination hardly matters. It is the expansion of our own understanding that is their chief significance. The discovery of the New World profoundly affected all aspects of the arts and literature in Europe in ways no one could have predicted; there was no hint that it even existed. The *auctores* of the theory of evolution in the nineteenth century, also unexpected, had a similar impact on modern thought and culture. If we look for the great *auctores* of the last century, there are few whose thinking ignited more wildly varied methods of analysis into all aspects of human behavior than Freud. What appeared in each instance was not a path, but a multitude of paths, in different directions, with no end in sight or expected. *The Interpretation of Dreams*, or *The Origin of Species*—or the Quran or the Tao te Ching—do more to shatter existing orthodoxies than to lay down new ones. These are works of such originality that the only fitting response to them among their students and disciples is to an achieve an originality of their own.

Auctoritas understood in this fashion is very close to what Plato called "poetry" (Gr. *poiesis*) in *The Republic*. The word "poet" for him included every kind of artist and artisan, from writers and actors to cosmetologists. As he saw it, all of the poets (*poietai*) were a danger to his carefully ordered *civitas*. Because they could present images of things that did not exist—that is, use their creative imagination—they could distort reality itself and cause false beliefs among the citizens, weakening the authority (power) of the philosopher-king. The imitative poet "is a manufacturer of images and is very far from the truth," thus heats the passions and "lets them rule, although they ought to be controlled, if mankind were ever to increase in happiness and virtue."[29] The *poietai* must therefore be exiled or instructed by the authorities as to exactly what they are to represent in their arts. Plato's Republic is a completely rational and comprehensive system. It is threatened more by the poets than by its military enemies—in fact, it *needs* those enemies.

The Christian gospels (the "good news," Gr. *Euangellion*) are especially notable instances of *auctoritas*, or *poiesis*. Note the inclusion of "angel" in the Greek word for gospel. Angels are messengers from an otherwise hidden place. There is no way of anticipating their disclosures. They come, we might say, out of nowhere. The three Magi who brought the news to King Herod were perfect strangers, coming from a distant and unnamed land. Whether their announcements were actually "good" was hardly evident at the time. In fact, for the most part they inspired profound dread. The shepherds to whom the angel reported the birth of the Christ child were terrified and left speechless. Herod, the narrative goes, was so alarmed by the news that he slaughtered all male infants under the age of two. This yet unborn child apparently was a greater threat to the grand belief system of Roman Palestine than all of its enemies combined. Observe that no one knew what these "tidings" *meant*. There was no obvious context within which to make sense of them. Indeed, Jesus himself made little sense to his entire age; even his own disciples missed the point, whatever the point was. In fact, this has proved to be an event *no one* understands.

Christianity is not the only religion in which this divine interruption was so unpredictable and often unintelligible. What can we make of the fact that the angel wrestled with Jacob through the night and only ceased when it was the *angel* who was injured? Krishna was notoriously unpredictable, at one moment appearing as a chariot driver urging Prince Arjuna to join in battle with his cousins, at another as a beautiful boy seducing milkmaids, as much trickster as god. The Buddha, and countless teachers following him, demonstrated a high skill of confounding questioners and leaving them with indecipherable tropes and mantras, the single clapping hand the best known of them.

There is a variety of corresponding practices that acknowledge the unreliability of the divine. Meditators, for example, sitting with hands open and turned upward, are in the act of receiving—without knowing what will be provided. But whatever comes, they do not walk away with fists closed as though now that the goal of meditation has been achieved, the insight received, it must not be allowed to escape. The incompleteness remains, the hands open.

Auctores, poietai, angels, bodhisattvas, avatars, gurus, ayatollahs, shamans are all authorities inasmuch as they are sources of unexpected wisdom. Together they share one striking characteristic: they are all at home in one or another belief system, but without being captive to it. The Buddha emerges from a distinctly Hindu context; Muhammad from a loose mixture of folk religion and fragments of Judaism and Christianity. Neither Kierkegaard nor Marx can be seen in isolation from Hegelianism, then the dominant belief system in the European universities at the time. And yet while each poet must have a home, its doors are open; in fact, it is they who open them.

Although poets exercise the freedom of opening doors, they are not enemies of their own or of any other belief system. Although they likely have a home within one bounded context or another, it is as a point of departure and not as a place of confinement. To be at home in a belief system does not imply that poets *belong* to it, as being identified with or possessed by it—unless, of course, they accede to the demands of the philosopher-king and create works that reinforce the state's restrictive authority.

Plato exiled poets, but not all of them. His use of poetry was to put it at the service of the *civitas,* disabling its unbounded horizonal visions. Ideologies that understand authority as power also understand that they need their poets, or propagandists. Writing heroic music or poetry, designing war monuments, painting flattering portraits of their rulers and scenes of national triumph, revising official histories, composing national anthems, arranging celebratory events, developing appropriate rituals, and, of course, composing an underpinning philosophy showing the rationality and necessity of the *civitas*—all are ways of neutering its poets.

It sometimes happens that the *civitas*'s poetry escapes its boundedness. Bertolt Brecht's plays, meant to underscore the need for a Marxist state, have transcended their origin to become works of art without a trace of ideology. Plato's *Republic,* a prescription for an airless society under the total control of its ruler and his soldiers, is itself a work of poetry so remarkable that it has broken free of any political strategy. Michelangelo, a markedly unpleasant and miserly fellow, putting himself in the pecuniary service of a pope whose belief system attempted to enclose an entire civilization, created works of art that elude all attempts to reduce them to their functional uses. But for the most part, official art is eminently forgettable. Soviet architecture and statuary are so formularized that even their creators remain anonymous. Vittorio Emanuele's colossal monument in Rome is so obscenely heroic and triumphant that it seems a mockery of the surrounding classical ruins.

The real danger poets represent lies not in their rejection of belief systems but in their indifference to them. Because they are not focused on disproving belief as such, they do not come with arguments. Poetry, it must be emphasized, does not translate into belief, or into rational thought of any kind. It can be little more than a random insight, or a puzzling oracular declaration. (What could be more irrational, or more poetic, than Freud's theory of the unconscious?) It need not always be verbal; it can just as easily be an action. Though indifferent to boundaries, poets are certainly aware of them. Believers may well be alarmed by an unexpected revelation of possibilities. But there is no hand-to-hand action that can be taken. To attack these revelations or oracles or visions is to stab at smoke. A common strategy for repelling them is the attempt to convert them into a belief system and then reject them. Look again at Charles Darwin. He was a furnace of new ideas, many woefully incomplete and frequently unsupported, but ideas so original and seminal that they have opened countless thinkers to new insights of their own. His were ideas that did not oppose, but goaded and inspired. Believers have long felt themselves threatened by what they thought

Darwin was saying and in fact created a kind of "Darwinian" ideology that they then simplified and made suitable for scorn. To be sure, many of his intellectual heirs have themselves staked out exclusive acreage, to make a home for orthodoxy. But the originating ideas have enough poetry in them that they cannot be captured; they persistently wander into other meadows.

The challenge faced by Plato's philosopher-king in the Republic was to use art as an extension of his own policies. He was not interested in art as such but only in purifying and freezing the *thinking* of his populace. (He was a *philosopher*-king, after all.) He requires both predictability and redundance. He decides *in advance* what the work of art will be. In other words, he must take the art out of the art. This all reveals something of the true nature of poetry, that is, every form of original expression from hairstyling and dramaturgy to oratory and ceramics. Poetry *says* nothing. It serves no ends. It is inherently original and cannot be imagined in advance. It is therefore always surprising, and often disturbing. In its purest form, poetry's only "meaning" lies in the creation of more poetry, the more that follows it the greater its achievement. Poetry is, therefore, not *about* anything. Heroic monuments, on the other hand, are most precisely and obviously about something, thus their creators' anonymity. If we could agree on what *Oedipus Rex* is about we could focus on the agreement and ignore the play. But the play defies replacement by anything besides itself. Freud did not discover its meaning; it was Freud who was inspired by Sophocles' unrepeatability.

Authority in the mode of poetry, therefore, is the key to understanding the nature of *communitas*. There is no blueprint by which *communitas* can be properly laid out, and no typical expression of itself. *Communitas* thrives on originality, and that can include everything from the way one mows the lawn or walks in public to manners of speech and modes of worship of one or another deity. There is no saying what forms it will take. As previously noted, *communitas* is always compatible with a fresh expression of itself. It can have a radically different appearance from one *civitas* to another but one appearance of it will never be in conflict with another. We cannot belong to one *communitas* or another because it is not there before it is expressed. We do not join it so much as we create it. *Civitas,* on the other hand, is always singular. Its identity consists in setting itself off from all others, by being in outright competition with them or in direct conflict.

The great religions, so long as they are distinguished from the belief systems that have tried to contain them, present the most complete expressions of *communitas.* In their purest forms, they are thoroughly poetic. Odd as it may seem so far, as richly verbal as religions are, like poetry *they say nothing.* There is no point to any of them. Not one of them is perfect, of course; each is vigorously threatened by the believers who attempt to lay claim to it. To whom, after all, does Islam or Buddhism belong? When they belong to something or someone outside themselves, they have become dead *qua* religions. Although they come closest of all human institutions to being pure poetry, that is, creations that have no prior blueprint, their imperfections are grave enough that in time each will die a death peculiar to itself, as countless religions already have. Just as art ceases to be art in totalitarian societies, religion ceases to be religion when its poetic authority is recast as civic authority. So far as America is understood as a

Christian nation, and Christianity as an American religion, each has given away its enormous vitality to a constricted and spiritless redundancy.

There is no more trenchant illustration of the perverted misuse of poetry by believers than the attack on the World Trade Center and the Pentagon. Nineteen pirates, seizing instruments of great technical sophistication, needing to create a display of their ideological certainties, succeeded in creating an artistic image so vivid it is certain never to be forgotten by civilized people. The brilliance of their imagination and execution cannot be exaggerated. The *factuality* of what occurred on that day, while truly horrible, was far less important than the poetry. It is mistakenly represented as a matter of numbers. While three thousand people died in the attack, three thousand more would die on American highways in the next three weeks. For several preceding decades, there have been the equivalent of some fifteen or twenty destroyed World Trade Centers *every year*. The economic consequences of 9/11 do not remotely compare to those of the highway carnage, with its medical bills, lost wages, and higher insurance rates. One can only imagine what difference it would make if the public were to press the government to spend three billion dollars each month to design and build safer cars and highways. So it was the poetry of the terrorists' achievement that has seized our attention so effectively to have drawn the nation into two devastating wars. They were perfectly dutiful servants of their philosopher-king. It was an act of so far unequaled propagandistic art. But because it was *poetry the end of which was not poetry*, that is, because it was a dazzling expression of a belief system so utterly closed, what it produced was an event of exceeding ugliness. It is a reminder that believers can employ extraordinary works of the imagination in the service of evil.

Authority as power, authority as poetry—two conceptions that appear to contradict each other in fact are one. The only difference is that the use of authority as power is possible only when we conceal from ourselves that it is we, and not some supreme independent agent, who have endowed a text or a person or an institution with power. This results in the irony that such authority is effective only when it is obedient to those who declare obedience to it. Those who so endow it can only do so in willful ignorance. The use of authority as poetry wears its ignorance fully in the open. This is what we see in Lincoln's Second Inaugural. More than halfway into the address, the North is presented as having won a moral victory, chiefly over the issue of slavery. "All knew that this interest was, somehow, the cause of the war." To this point, Lincoln is offering little more than the usual claim that not only did the enemy start the war but all its evils lay on their side. So far, he has kept God out of it. When God does enter, we are surprised to learn that although the victory may be moral, there is no ground for calling it righteous. Although both sides read the same Bible and pray to the same God, it is still the case that "the Almighty has his own purposes." With this simple sentence, all human authority has just been faulted. We do not in fact know what we are doing, even when it has to do with such terrible ills as slavery. If "all the wealth piled by the bondsman's two hundred and fifty years of unrequited toil shall be sunk," it is nonetheless true that, as the psalmist said, "the judgments of the Lord are true and righteous altogether." A stronger assault on human certitude and absolutism cannot be made. American triumphalism in any of its possible forms is nothing more than an enormous work of willful ignorance. Lincoln is the greatest of the nation's poets.

Assigning to belief an essentially voluntary character, in spite of the claim that it originates in a source outside oneself, seems to lead straight into relativism—where nothing is absolutely true and anything can be believed. But some boundaries are necessary; the issue is the degree to which they are permeable. If they are perfectly sealed, belief systems will choke on their own breath. Like the skin of the body, there must be some commerce between what is contained and what is excluded. *Boundary* must therefore be balanced with *horizon*. A horizon is the outer edge of our vision. Beyond it we see nothing. However, to move toward it in any direction is to bring something new into sight. What this will be cannot be known beforehand. Boundary serves to establish the *civitas*, a society that sets rational standards for its essential functions. Horizon leads to and results from the existence of the *communitas*, a collection of persons who assist each other in extending their common field of vision. *Civitas* and *communitas* are both dependent on their authorities, but authorities very differently conceived. For one, authority has an essentially ordering role and is granted the power to act out its role. It does not seize power, even if it makes violent moves to do so, but rules only on the consent of those its rules. For the other, authority does not come in the form of power, but of poetry (*poiesis*). Authorities are those who come from outside the known horizons with visions of territories so far unknown; they lead not by ruling but by the act of *author*-ship. They are poets in the Platonic sense of giving birth to new thoughts and knowledge that might be dangerous to the order of the *civitas*. Poets are not believers. Their poetry does not translate into beliefs. Outside *communitas* their contributions may be meaningless, or even invisible; within *communitas* they enliven the conversation of its members with one another, leading them to deeper and less decipherable unknowns. The end of poetry is therefore poetry itself.

PART II
RELIGION

We now leave the relatively tidy terrain of belief systems with their tended walls and delineated enemies for the more complicated, often foggy, sometimes hidden, and increasingly varied geography of religion. It might seem strange to leave belief behind when the discussion of religion itself begins, since religion is popularly thought to be the exclusive precinct of believers. It may appear that what is coming will be an unconventional view of what it means to be religious. That is partly correct, but what I intend to show is that in all of the great religions belief takes a diminished place, if any at all, and is very often a sign that whatever counts for religion has been pushed aside. Therefore the task of offering a definition of religion can no longer be delayed.

Religion in its purest form is a vast work of poetry. As such, its vitality comes in the form of *communitas*, fully independent of any one *civitas* or another. The claim badly needs a historical example. While we can find lively forms of ignorance in almost all religious phenomena, there is one that, for its extremes, stands larger than all the others: the life of Jesus of Nazareth as he is pictured in the New Testament, Christian history, modern scholarship, and popular literature. He is easily the most enigmatic figure in human history: a homeless and quite likely illiterate wanderer, known to us only for what he said and did during the last months of his short life, but believed by several billion of his followers to be God incarnate. How does this man, and the religion that grew around him, reveal the extent to which we do not know what we do not know? How does it shatter the certainty of believers in a way that does not drive them off but leaves them in a state of wonder? The challenge here is to show how the vast literature on Jesus is *not about anything*; that, in fact, it *says nothing*. Indeed, that saying nothing, perhaps more profoundly than any other work of poetry, is its glory.

There is only one reliable extratestamental reference to Jesus's existence. It is found in the work of a puzzling figure: Flavius Josephus (37–c. 100 CE). Although retired as a Roman general who had participated in the final destruction of Jerusalem, Josephus was himself a Jew who began his military career fighting the Romans. By rare good fortune and skillful manipulation he came to be an honored citizen of Rome, in which city he spent his final years composing two large volumes, *The Jewish War*, covering the years 66–73, and *The Antiquities of the Jews*, a history that begins with the creation and ends with the war. The latter book contains a brief reference to Jesus. The text has been considerably muddied by attempts of later translators and scribes to add manifestly theological references—clearly unattributable to Josephus himself. Rinsed of these inserts (indicated by the elisions), we find Josephus describing Jesus as "a wise man . . . a doer of startling deeds, a teacher of people who receive the truth with pleasure."[1] He reports that Pilate condemned him to the cross—for an unspecified crime—but "those who loved him did not cease to do so. . . . And up to this very day the tribe of Christians, who loved him, has not died out." Although these several sentences make up but a tiny portion of the four hundred pages of Josephus's account of the age, they at least offer persuasive evidence of the man's existence.[2]

Within the New Testament itself there is enough historical detail, such as references to Caesar Augustus, King Herod, and Pontius Pilate, to locate the events related in a specific time and place with confidence.[3] Most of the authors of the New Testament material wrote without direct knowledge of the others, but collectively their references to known events coordinate quite convincingly.[4] Therefore, we know with some certainty that the man existed, but what do we know *about* the man? For this, we must rely initially on the New Testament itself. Later, other data, drawn from archaeology and a close reading of non-Christian literature of the time, have added details to the portrait of Jesus without substantively altering its New Testament design.

There are twenty-seven books in the New Testament. The gospels of Matthew, Mark, Luke, John, and the book of Acts (also written by Luke) take up approximately half of it. Of these authors essentially nothing is known beyond their names—and even their names were honorifics added in the late second century. They were most certainly not eyewitnesses of the events they describe, nor do they present themselves as such. The gospels are written in the form of the "lives," or *bioi*, of prominent men, a style common to the age. The book of Acts is written as a history of the period immediately after Jesus's death and resurrection, and the events surrounding the first (mostly unsuccessful) efforts to draw together a harmonious Christian community. The remaining literature is mostly that of letters varying in length, purpose, and point of view. The seven letters of Paul are by far the most dominant of these. The final piece is the book of Revelation, a series of visions with so little connection to the rest of the New Testament or, for that matter, any other known literary or religious work that it is difficult to know how to weigh its importance.

As a work of literature, the New Testament has no unifying style and genre. Not only is it a pastiche of gospel, history, epistle, and vision, but its writers vary in geographical location, intellectual and religious background, theological disposition, and levels of narrative and expository skills. Moreover, the individual parts were written over a period of at least thirty years, approximately from 70 to 100 CE. Not only were none of the writers eyewitnesses of the events reported, most of them could not have known such a witness. Even more, Jesus spoke Aramaic, the evangelists Greek. He was Jewish, they were mostly gentile. His entire ministry takes place within the few miles that extend from Galilee to Jerusalem, not more than a two days' walk. They were dispersed throughout the Middle East and probably never visited Jerusalem. They were members of rival Christian churches, institutions Jesus could not possibly have known, or no doubt could not even have imagined.

Looking more closely at the text, the picture becomes even more confusing, as we can see from a few examples. Of the four gospels, that of John is usually set apart from the others. In what could not be a greater departure from the popular narratives of Jesus's birth in Matthew and Luke, John opens his gospel with magisterial abstraction: "In the beginning was the word and the word was with God and the word is God" (1:1). And a few verses later: "And the word became flesh and dwelt among us, full of grace and truth" (1:14). Although the subsequent narrative contains sufficient detail of his full humanity (only in this gospel does Jesus actually weep, at learning of the death of his friend Lazarus: 11:35),[5] we are often reminded of his divine nature: "I am the resurrection and the life; he who believes in me, though he die, yet shall he live" (11:25–26). If the *person* of Jesus in the gospel of John departs significantly from that of the other gospels, so does his *teaching*. While they have their Jesus speaking of the law, the conduct of the spiritual life, and the coming kingdom of God, the Jesus of the fourth gospel is himself the subject of his teaching, declaring, for example, that "I am the way and the truth and the life; no one comes to the Father, but by me" (14:6). Were John's Jesus and the Jesus of the Synoptics to meet, they would not recognize each other.

But then we can hardly find a consistent picture of the Jesus of the first three gospels. Some of the textual contradictions are startling. Matthew's Jesus is born in Bethlehem, where he lived to the age of two, when Herod is said to have begun his enraged slaughter of the innocents, alarmed by the oracular announcement of three mysterious visitors that a rival king had been born (1:18ff.). The young family then fled to Egypt, returning only when they learned of Herod's death, settling in Nazareth. The parents of Luke's Jesus, by contrast, lived in Nazareth and shortly before Jesus was born traveled to Bethlehem to register in a census (2:1ff.). There is no mention of the slaughter or the exile in Egypt. One can almost picture the two families passing each other on the road. In the meantime, the older gospel of Mark, like that of John, shows no interest in the birth of Jesus whatsoever. His account opens on the baptism of the adult Jesus by the figure identified only as John the Baptizer. Nothing here about shepherds, a birth among animals, a flight to safety, soothsayers from the East, angelic announcements, or even the virgin birth.

As we scroll through the gospel texts the inconsistencies and enigmas continue to multiply. Citing a few will suffice. In the first three gospels, Jesus's entire ministry occurs within one year's time; in the fourth gospel it is three years. There are also substantial variations in Jesus's last words on the cross. In Matthew and Mark, he cries with a loud voice, "My God, my God, why hast thou forsaken me?" (27:46; 15:35). In Luke, he cries, "Father, into thy hands I commit my spirit" (23:46), and in John a much more subdued, "It is finished" (19:30; a single word in Greek). What's more, the empty tomb is discovered variously by one woman, two women, and three. For that matter, where are the many thousands who were said to have attended his teaching and witnessed his miracles only a few weeks earlier? Although there is considerable agreement among all four gospels on the details of the trial, the resurrection narratives scatter the appearances of the risen Lord, some in Galilee, and some in Jerusalem. It gets no better when we get to Acts or to Paul. Paul obviously knew of some of the material recorded in the gospels, but even he tells of an appearance of the risen Christ first to Peter, then to "the twelve," and then to "the five hundred" (1 Cor. 15:3–8), events that are apparently unknown to any other New Testament writer.[6]

There are scores of additional textual confusions, but no need to add to the list; any attentive reader can easily discover them.[7] Indeed, the relative unreliability of the text for drawing a complete picture of Jesus was known to the evangelists themselves. The author of the fourth gospel concludes with the remark, "There are many other things which Jesus did; were every one of them to be written, I suppose the world itself could not contain the books that would be written" (21:25). Luke, too, refers to the many who "have undertaken to compile a narrative of the things which were accomplished among us" (1:1). The obvious implication is that the Christian community was abounding in gospels and recollections, of which scarcely a trace has survived. The unknown editors and compilers of the New Testament documents were themselves aware of the selective use of sources by its writers.

All of this gives the strong impression that the New Testament as we have it is a somewhat errant representation of a true text that hovers somewhere behind it, unseen, even unseeable— a precise and accurate account of what Jesus said and did. Apparently no one is granted the talent or privilege to state it exactly as it is. As a result, we remain necessarily ignorant of the "true" text. It is inconceivable that Christians will someday reach total agreement on what that text may be. However far we proceed in our understanding of Jesus as the New Testament presents him, a horizon remains, and what lies beyond it cannot be imagined.

No doubt this is why the first four books of the New Testament are not called "The Gospel," but "The Gospel According to —." It is as though every scholar, preacher, and believer are not to declare, "This is the man Jesus," without adding the qualifying, "as far as I know."

In sum, this is enough to say that, *as a work of literature*, the New Testament is extremely difficult to characterize. It is hardly surprising that for centuries scholars have been trying to improve on it, ironing out its contradictions, explaining away its divergences, focusing on one bit of the text at the exclusion of the rest, isolating the harmonious parts for separate publication. But the confusion is too extensive. It reaches so far into itself that all such scholarly attempts to clean it up are certain to fail. Uncertainty is sewn into the faith from the beginning.

However, if as a work of literature the New Testament is confused, *as a work of religious literature* it's a glorious confusion. Its abiding power lies precisely in the fact that every attempt to improve it is doomed. If this is a collection of assorted writings that fights off every effort to make it into something other than what it is, it is also a work so engagingly annoying and disturbing that it draws armies of interpreters into its silken net of limitless possibilities. And leaves them there. In the dark. Quarreling with one another. Or quarreling with the text. It matters not in the least to the text whether the reader comes as its champion or its detractor. That they are drawn to it at all is sufficient proof of its apparently inexhaustible vitality.

So we have a choice. We can continue to shout down the offending voices until we hear something that echoes our preferred composition, or we can join in to make a joyful noise of our own. We can read it for what we think it says, or we can read it for what it allows us to say. We can regard the text as definitive, containing all we need to know, or as generative, leading beyond itself to what is not yet known.

The generative power of the quest for the "real" Jesus is abundantly evident in the two thousand years of Christian history where countless scholars and theologians have tried to draw out a definitive understanding of the man. Altogether the effort must be seen as an extraordinary work of the imagination, a long creative train of innovations, or successive visions. The tradition has not always been pretty. Death by fire, torture, exile, imprisonment, excommunication, and general scorn have too frequently greeted original insights into the person of Jesus. But these punishments have done little to silence them. To the present day, novel readings of the text have outrun all attempts to channel or contain them.

As an echo of John's famous remark about the vast written and oral library of stories about Jesus, it is not only beyond the scope of this book to summarize the attempts to come to clarity on the "real" Jesus, it is beyond the scope of any book, even whole libraries of books. But a few examples can indicate with how much variety Christians, and their resisting nonbelievers, have been trying to set down a coherent, relevant, and convincing picture.

If there is a dominant theme in the successive attempts to capture him, it lies in the emphatic testimony of the New Testament that although he is thoroughly human, he is also divine. But the New Testament does little to help us understand how these two natures are related. The theological tradition was not slow in offering a variety of solutions. Some thought that he only *appeared* to be human (Docetism); others that he was human enough but that the divine communicated through him without creating a union (Nestorianism). One widely held theory was that he lived such an unblemished life as a naturally born human being that God chose him as his son (Adoptionism). By radically emphasizing the divine nature in Jesus, another theological view was that Jesus and God are essentially one person (Monophysitism). The claim that he was divine all right but of a degree lower than God, and in fact created by God (Arianism), became controversial enough that it was dividing Christendom.

Augustine, bishop of Hippo in North Africa (354–430), and probably the most influential thinker in Christian history, held firmly to the view that Jesus was of two natures, divine and human, each perfect in itself. It is a stretch to find anything in the New Testament that explicitly claims this, and Augustine did little to explain how it could even be possible.[8] Nonetheless he defined the framework within which successive writers were to be judged orthodox in describing their Jesuses. Of course, even Augustine's massive authority would be repeatedly defied.

In the meantime, other ways of describing the person of Jesus were developing in the early church. Irenaeus, the bishop of Lyons (130–202), taking as a clue Paul's reference to Jesus as the Second Adam, offered an agile scheme that described Jesus's life as a "recapitulation" of Adam's, reversing the effects of his fall into sin. As Adam ate of the forbidden tree, Jesus was crucified on a tree; as Adam died, so did Jesus; as Adam was expelled from paradise, Jesus wandered in the wilderness, resisting the temptations of Satan—all with the result of cleansing the race of its hopeless condemnation.[9]

Skipping to the other end of the first Christian millennium, Anselm, bishop of Canterbury (d. 1109), presented a Jesus who is nowhere found in the New Testament and who would have seemed peculiar, if not bizarre, to Augustine and Irenaeus. Anselm was a powerful thinker and has sometimes been called the "father of scholasticism," for giving shape to both philosophical and theological thinking of the Middle Ages. His most famous and consequent work, *Cur Deus Homo*, or *Why the God-man*, is a classic example of scholastic thought inasmuch as he sets out to show the error of nonbelievers who reject Christianity "because they regard it as contrary to reason."[10] For him, however, "the will of God is never irrational."[11] He intends to show that the incarnation of God in Christ was absolutely necessary—by reason alone. His argument is spare and to the point. God created Adam and Eve to live perfect lives, but since they freely disobeyed their creator, they, and the human race that descended from the pair, are condemned to eternal death. But such a condemnation is in fact a contradiction of the goodness of God by which he created them. Anselm presents God as caught in a dilemma: either he overlooks the offense, which is an unacceptable blemish on his own being, or he lets the judgment stand, in which case his beloved children will suffer dreadfully. The children themselves are helpless because no matter how well they live, their collective indebtedness to God for their offense against him is far beyond anything they can afford. "If I owe him myself and all that I can do," Anselm says in the voice of a believer, "even when I do not sin, I have nothing to repay for sin."[12] But "while no one save God can make [the payment] and no one save man ought to make it, it is necessary for a God-man to make it."[13]

Since the man Jesus in whom God is incarnate is flawless, since Jesus freely chooses to give up his life for our sake, and since the value of his life—it being both human and divine—far exceeds any debt owed by us, and since he has done this out of love, not judgment, he gladly pays the debt on our behalf. God has redeemed his children without shame to himself and without compromising their humanity—or his rationality.

Anselm's solution is certainly ingenious, but the heavenly exchange of merits seems to occur in another time and place, far outside the experience of the believers for whom the redemption is made. By what means do we connect ourselves to the redeeming labors of Jesus?

Anselm is deeply influenced by Plato and his transcendent realm of pure ideas. The emergence of Aristotelian thought in the following centuries raised a very different problem for interpreting the life of Jesus, and offered a very different solution, especially as it was elaborated in the magnificent theological system of Thomas Aquinas. Aristotle starts with experience, not ideas. His is an empirical world where what is true must first come to us through the senses. If there is no experiential grounding to our ideas, they drift off, detached from reality. This way of thinking had a profound effect on Christendom. We see it chiefly in the emphasis on the *sacramental* relation of the believer to Jesus. The seven sacraments—baptism; the Eucharist, or Last Supper; marriage; last rites; ordination; confession; and confirmation—were thought to be established by Jesus himself as a way of providing believers with a tangible access to his living being. Although it is difficult to find the origin of all of these rites in the New Testament (baptism and the Eucharist, or Last Supper, are the two most explicitly supported by the text), it is still the case that they came to be the center of the lives of centuries of Christians.

Critics of the sacramental church, especially the Protestants, saw it as a mechanical affair where the mere repetition of the designated rites worked their effects on the worshiper—regardless of the worshiper's own state of mind. The criticism misses the point. Each of the sacraments has a physical component: water, bread, wine, oil, and in one case, the sound of the human voice. By means of these most ordinary substances, as plain as reality gets, the plenitude of divine existence becomes existentially real in our lives: a true marriage of the infinite and the finite.

One of the consequences of sacramental thinking is that since the events of the New Testament and the experience of the believer are so directly linked, and since the administration of the sacraments is limited exclusively to the church hierarchy, the church in effect makes itself the historical extension of Christ, as though no time has passed between the earthly life of Jesus and the earthly life of the believer. The church, in other words, can speak for Jesus. To go to Jesus is to go to the church, that is, to the church hierarchy.

Although sacramentalism finds scant justification in the New Testament, it must be admitted that it is another way of reading the text that makes it sensibly useful. For Martin Luther, however, identification of the church with Jesus blocked the Christian's path to Jesus. The church's faulted human character, with all of its arrogance and self-interested scheming, fractured the connection to Jesus that the sacraments were thought to provide. As we have seen, his derision of the pope and the church's officers is notorious, leading him to go so far as to refer to the pope by name as "Jack Sausage" (*Hans Wurst*). But Luther's deeper reason for his opposition to the church was simply that it was unnecessary. Whatever means by which we can be in the presence of Jesus, or what Paul called being "in Christ," we already have in scripture. The Bible is not merely a collection of histories and teachings; it is the Word, the means by which God has chosen to enter the lives of his children. The Word, as spoken by God, is contained in scripture but it is not identical to it. That Word, as the gospel of John plainly declares it, has become flesh. What God *says* through the text is in fact the incarnate Lord. If the expression seems odd, it is only because Luther has taken the Johannine text to its extreme. But he also has Paul's expression, "faith comes by hearing," to support his reading. The decisive factor here is that in hearing (or reading) the Word we can receive it in its entirety. No priest or scholar or authority of any kind is necessary.

For all the scriptural integrity of Luther's interpretation of the biblical Jesus, there is a danger in its extremes. By shifting the authority of both church and tradition to the individual listener, those who hear the Word can interpret it any way they wish. There is no external restraint on their beliefs or actions. One Jesus is as authentic as the next. There were several dramatic results to this way of thinking. Even in Luther's own lifetime there was an explosive growth in the varieties of interpretation. In what is known as the Radical Reformation, Christians, liberated from ecclesiastical restraints, formed groups around novel and idiosyncratic, often bizarre interpretations; some even formed utopian communities, all of which perished in violent conflict

with the larger society. The other consequence of Luther's reformation is found in the Peasants' War (1524–26), a brutal and
apparently spontaneous uprising aimed at both the ruling gentry
and the church's large monastic holdings. It may be too much to
say that the war—the largest uprising of its kind until the French
Revolution—is the direct result of the Reformation, but there is
no doubt that much of the fervor of the badly armed but bold
armies of peasants was owed largely to Luther's pen. In both instances, Luther was himself horrified by these events and began
to insist on more institutional control. But it was too late. The
fracturing of Protestantism into a broad spectrum of sects had
begun, and Luther's fears that it would never end have been well
justified. To this day, his rebellion spawns a dismaying multitude
of sects and divisions of the church that often bear little resemblance to one another.

Luther's co-reformer, John Calvin, rejected papal authority
on much the same grounds. But his reading of the Bible was
much less radical. For him Jesus was to be understood in a more
substantive reading of the text, including the Old Testament.
Calvin followed the practice of assigning Jesus to three roles:
prophet (or teacher, in which he himself is the teaching), priest
(in which he himself is the sacrifice), and king (the final judge).
Calvin's successors, in contrast to Luther's, were less moved by
the inherent irrationality of Christianity and more disposed toward institutional solidity and large positive systems of "systematic" theology.

These systems wilted quickly under the scrutiny of philosophers in the Enlightenment period. The German Jewish thinker
Gotthold Ephraim Lessing asked the damning question: given the

unreliability of historical evidence, how can we go back across "the broad, ugly ditch of history" to prove the eternal fact that Jesus was also God?[14] Kant let the question of Jesus's divinity slide, describing him as an example of perfect morality.[15] Even Thomas Jefferson contributed to this revision of the Jesus of history by scissoring out (literally) the passages of the gospels he found objectionable—namely, all intimations of Jesus's divinity—and titling what remained *The Life and Morals of Jesus of Nazareth*.[16] In a far more radical revision, Hegel tucked the historical Jesus into a vast scheme by which the eternal One alienates itself from itself, thus creating history, as a means of reconciling itself to itself as a perfect Unity. Could Matthew and Luke have seen *any* resemblance of this Jesus to their own?

The Dane Søren Kierkegaard (1813–55) thought he could employ that very Enlightenment skepticism, and a revision of the Hegelian dialectic, to take us back to the eternal Jesus of history. Kierkegaard asserted emphatically that the meeting of God and man in the person of Jesus not only made no sense, but could only be understood as the "absolute paradox." But how are we to relate to such a paradox? Reason will not undo it, neither will historical evidence. We have nothing but the mere claim that there once was a man, fully human like you and me, who was also God. There is no way we can get to the truth of this claim through the "chatter" of history, or across Lessing's ugly, broad ditch. Our only option is to hold fast to the "objective uncertainty" that this man was God, with "*an appropriate process of the most passionate inwardness.*" Faith is that most passionate inwardness. It is "the highest truth attainable of an *existing* individual."[17] The inward leap is into the unintelligible, into what

Nietzsche called the "abyss." But for Kierkegaard this was not a loss but the very highest stage of life itself.

Kierkegaard was largely ignored in his own century. While he was composing his remarkably original picture of Jesus, a very different theological movement was under way, one that had a far wider effect on the nineteenth century. A series of French and German scholars, no strangers to Enlightenment skepticism, thought that it was nonetheless possible to piece together a coherent life of Jesus by way of sophisticated textual analysis. Known as the *Leben Jesu*, or Life of Jesus, movement, it dominated Christian literature of the period. It came to an effective end with the publication of Albert Schweitzer's trenchant classic *The Quest for the Historical Jesus* in 1906, written before his achieving fame as a medical missionary in Africa. His aim was simple enough: to determine whether the scholarly labors of the *Leben Jesu* school succeeded in reaching consensus on a reliable biography. He found that, in spite of the high quality of their work, there were irreconcilable differences in the results. In one of the most prophetic comments in twentieth-century Christian literature, he concluded that Jesus "comes to us as one unknown, without a name, as of old, by the lakeside, [when] he came to those men who knew him not."[18]

The number and variety of Jesuses appearing in the twentieth century, especially in the Americas, easily prove that the aquifer is not dry. In fact, for all the scholarly brilliance of the preceding Christian tradition, the century produced a surprisingly fresh and novel supply. Consider the following, randomly selected from an indeterminate number: a world-reforming messenger of the kingdom of God, which he was determined to translate into something resembling a nineteenth-century socialist utopia;[19] a divinely appointed son of the god who, some six thousand years ago, fashioned the earth in six days then all but destroyed it fifteen hundred years later in a worldwide flood resulting in such phenomena as the Grand Canyon;[20] a mysterious Galilean preacher whose proclamation to the world (or *kerygma*), although encased in mythic thinking we know now to be false, still causes us to confront our own inauthenticity;[21] a pop icon and rock music sensation as "Superstar";[22] a pure-blooded and exemplary Aryan, first member of the Master Race;[23] a messiah who magically transports himself to the Americas after his resurrection in Jerusalem, speaking a language and describing a holy life only vaguely resembling the gospels of the New Testament;[24] a black man who has "the blood of all races in his veins";[25] a fun-loving, partygoing preacher of joy who happens also to be a paragon of efficient business discipline, a master advertiser, and in effect the founder of the modern corporation;[26] the representative in relatively modern history of an omnipotent but secretive craftsman who billions of years ago assembled a universe that has been evolving since in a process of clockwork perfection;[27] an agent of God whose life on earth, dedicated to the salvation of the human race from sin, was only partly successful and who must therefore return to call his faithful children home in a dramatic event referred to as the "rapture";[28] an obscure itinerant preacher and wonderworker who once lived in the Galilee, something of a commercial and cultural crossroad, preaching a message not particularly distinct from the Judaism in which he was raised, whose reported resurrection is most certainly fictional;[29]

a blondish long-haired and blue-eyed non-Semite staring at us slightly off camera, a bit sad-faced but unmarked by suffering, and dressed in elegant and freshly laundered robes;[30] an enigmatic figure who, according to the best current scholarship, is properly to be understood as a "Jewish peasant Cynic";[31] a singing, dancing incarnation of ecstasy;[32] a man of the people who confronts the political, social, economic, racial, and sexual policies of a repressive capitalist culture;[33] a merciless military commander whose army crushes the forces of Satan on the plains of Israel (known also as Armageddon), then casts the losing generals into a blazing hole that opens just after he rejects their pleas for mercy;[34] a private voice guiding elected leaders responsible for America's salvific mission to the nondemocratic world.[35] This is not to mention more trivial suggestions that we consider Jesus as shaman, user of hallucinogenic mushrooms, homosexual, Maoist, father of secret children, Roman spy, pharisee, dupe of political powers, extraordinary athlete, carpenter on a year's sabbatical, member of the Essene cult, protomystic, Egyptian, spirit traveler to India, psychic, one's favorite philosopher, deluded victim of a messianic complex, avatar of Krishna, and just plain fictional, nothing more than an imagined character in a children's story.

This almost comic parade of Jesus interpreters is perhaps best characterized by the work of the last century's most celebrated theologian: Karl Barth. The ebullient Professor Barth found enough in the New Testament and its centuries of interpreters that needed clarification and correction to fill twelve volumes of his *Church Dogmatics*, totaling more than 7,750 pages, and a great number of other books and articles, bringing the whole to more than 10,000 pages, altogether some 500 times the length of the gospel of Mark. All this the result of the acts and words of a homeless illiterate.

So can we find the "real" Jesus? The question answers itself. Although many of these Jesuses are compatible with one or several others, none of them is a perfect resemblance, and most are so unlike the others that it seems only accidental that they have the same name. Indeed, each of them would consider all of the others impostors. All these Jesuses are there, of course, only because they have been invited by someone who believes they are real. They are not therefore the images of Jesus himself so much as they are the images projected by this believer or that.

What can we say but that everyone is wrong? The vast libraries of books, essays, and sermons composed about the man are but an accumulation of errors. It is true that *some* of it may be right, but there is no way finally of knowing. Essentially there is nothing everyone can agree to, beyond the reasonable fact that there was a man called Jesus. What is almost completely overlooked by both amateur and professional interpreters is that one consistent feature of the New Testament Jesus is that he is homeless; that is, he lived *in the open*. He was a public figure. Nothing about him was hidden. He was there in plain sight for everyone to see. This makes it all the more remarkable, and revealing, that we *still* cannot agree on what everyone was shown in the man. Given that Christians make up roughly a third of the world's population, and that a good portion of the remainder is at least familiar with the name of Jesus, he is, we must say, the most misunderstood and enigmatic person who ever lived. He is both the best known and the least known of all human beings. He is that person about whom the most has been said and about whom we are the most ignorant. As time passes, as research and speculation continue, so does our ignorance. Because it is impossible to think that the invention of new Jesuses will cease, or that someone will at last have the definitive concluding word, the sphere of this ignorance is bound to expand. About the man Jesus, much is *believed*, almost nothing is *known*.

It seems, therefore, that the image of the "quest" for the real Jesus, the idea that we can go somewhere to find him, has been reversed. Far from trying to get closer to him, we are moving outward along with a scattered community of other searchers. Whoever this person was and whatever he did in that final year of his short life, there was enough power there to set off a tsunami of ignorance. What does it mean then to "believe" in Jesus, or "believe" that Jesus was God, or to "believe" that he was *not* God, or that he was anything else? It means at the very least that we have to hide from ourselves how much we do not know; we have to call in our selected Jesus and close the door against the clamorous horde of alternative Jesuses surrounding our enclosure. But the roar won't diminish. No matter how successfully we deafen ourselves and suppress our curiosity, the excluded voices are always there to be heard by those who can hear. Not all voices are equal, of course. Some will rise above the others, drawing a larger audience, even requiring their own exposition, and deepening the wonder and the mystery of the man. It is in this sense that the vast literature about Jesus is *about nothing* except itself, and therefore ultimately *says nothing*. There is no possibility of standing back and declaring, "Ah, so this is what it is all about." To do so is only to join the clamor; it is to be taken over by the poetry of it all.

Jesus is not the only person around whom a cloud of ignorance forms. The names of others are quite familiar; indeed, the degree of their familiarity is an indication of the depth of our ignorance about them. We know a great deal, and yet nothing, about the Buddha. When will we ever get exactly the right understanding of Moses, or Muhammad, or Shankara, or Lao-tse? Or coming closer, when will the final word be written on Shakespeare, by far the most written-about literary figure in all human history, or Lincoln, the most written-about figure in American history?

It is just as true about all of these as it is about Jesus that their interpreters have not yet completely understood them. The more that is learned, the more the range of the unknown extends. The inability to settle on a final reading of any of them is not a matter of being historically or intellectually inaccurate. When interpreters claim certainty, declare that they have the "real" Jesus and the "true" teachings of Muhammad, *they are not making a factual but a religious mistake*. Why "religious"? What after all *is* religion?

The interest in defining religion as such arises with any prominence first in the Enlightenment of seventeenth- and eighteenth-century Europe, a time when acquaintance with the religions of Asia and the Middle East was rapidly expanding. It was, and still is, largely a Western, one might even say Christian, effort. The word is of Latin origin (*religio*) and nothing like it is found in Greek, Hebrew, and Arabic.[36] The earliest attempts at definition were driven by the desire to find a rational core to all systems of thought, including religious belief. The presumption was that at ground all such systems were not only intelligible but also compatible, as if underneath them all was a single body of truth in which each of them participates, if incompletely. There is still the popular idea that "all religions are one." Nowhere is this more baldly claimed than in the writings of Mahatma Gandhi. "I believe in the fundamental truth of all great religions of the world. . . . And I believe that, if only we could all of us read the scriptures of the different faiths from the stand-point of the followers of those faiths, we should find that they were at bottom all one and were all helpful to one another."[37] Interpreters more scholarly than Gandhi have taken the same approach.[38]

The closer scholars look, the more irreconcilable the different religions appear. Another tack seemed at first more promising: finding a need or a proclivity in each human being for religion of some kind. Already in the sixteenth century, John Calvin said that each of us by nature is a *fabricator deorum*, a maker of gods. In the nineteenth, the greatly learned Friedrich Schleiermacher spoke of religion rising from a "feeling of absolute dependence." Alfred North Whitehead's memorable remark is that religion is what "we do with our solitariness."[39] Rudolf Otto proposed that we each have a sense of being faced with a "mysterium tremendum" that leads to all forms of religion.[40] Paul Tillich's familiar phrase is that religion is an expression of our "ultimate concern."[41] These too, and many like them, are overly abstract and so widely applicable that they do little to account for the enormous variety within and among the great religions.

Notice how these attempts to define religion imply one kind of *experience* or another: feeling of absolute dependence, ultimate concern, solitariness. Kierkegaard, as we saw, considered faith "an act of passionate inwardness." The problem of religious experience seems especially to intrude in discussions of religion as a generic. It should be kept out of them. In the first place, it implies that there is one thing, and one thing only, that qualifies as genuine experience. This is especially true of the most famous and influential study of the subject: William James's *The Varieties of Religious Experience.* James analyzed a number of firsthand accounts of believers, hoping to clarify exactly what is meant by the term. This approach has several problems. Looking for the archetypal religious experience is analogous to a search for the singular experience of being married, or working in a corporation, or competing in an athletic event. What it means to be a parent or an athlete cannot be condensed into a single moment or even a series of them. In the second place, as is evident in James's definition, most attempts to isolate the distinctive character of religious experience are focused on the individual and not the larger *communitas* of which the individual is a part. To be religious in Tibet, as a Buddhist, has little in common with being an evangelical in Brazil. All experience is context specific. As our communal contexts change so does our experience within them. Third, there is a problem with isolating any experience as a momentary event distinct from what comes before and after. Scoring a goal in the final seconds of the game, giving your team the victory, has a texture quite unlike a score in the first half of a practice game. Experiences do not have sharp edges. When they begin and end cannot be marked by the second hand on a clock. Although it makes no sense to find one experience that can be called religious, *there is a religious element in every experience.* Over the course of a lifetime, experiences we thought were fixed and identifiable can come to be quite differently perceived. What may seem unambiguous to a bride during the ceremony will look very different from her perspective as wife, and mother, and widow. Experiences are infinitely reinterpretable; they are open-ended, each penetrated by its unknown consequences, each a fit occasion for wonder.

In fact, the inapplicability of conventional definitions underscores the great variety of religious expression and practice. Nothing quite fits over the whole because the whole has too many differences within itself to be covered by a single definition, even by a single description. It is because of these differences that a once influential approach to the study of religion was to *compare* one with another. Comparative religion, an active academic enterprise for most of the last century, has also been found dismayingly inadequate, if possible at all. In a widely influential essay on the essential failure of comparative religion,[42] Jonathan Z. Smith, a prominent historian and philosopher of religion, challenges the very idea of comparison itself. He observes that "comparison, at base, is not identity." One thing might be *like* another, but cannot *be* another. So who is to say what the difference is? Obviously, every interpreter will see a different likeness, or unlikeness, without any objective ground for deciding whether it is appropriate.[43] Why should we think that comparing and contrasting the ritual practices of several religions has any priority over, say, an analysis of the theological implications in their sacred scriptures? Smith's conclusion is stark: although he himself sees no solution to the problem, the very "possibility of the study of religion depends on its answer."[44] If we do not know how to compare religions, we do not know how to study them—as religions. Responding scholars concede his point, but still they feel some kind of comparison is possible, even if it is negative, in the sense that we can agree to mutual misunderstanding with a member of another religion. This is a response more wistful than helpful.

But even this diminished effort faces the difficulty of our not knowing exactly what is to be compared. When we use the term "religion," we usually have certain phenomena or traditions in mind, chief among them Hinduism, Buddhism, Judaism, Christianity, and Islam. Referring to these as religions is for the most part unobjectionable. The word gets a bit more vague when it comes to, say, Sikhism, Shinto, Confucianism, Taoism, Deism, Mormonism, Bahai, and Transcendentalism. Which of these is a candidate for comparison? Centuries of scholarly quarreling over the definition of religion, with no resolution in sight or even imaginable, take us to the conclusion that religion is not only undefinable, but that *we cannot say what religion is.* Before we go to study a "religion," we have no clear way of deciding that it is even a religion. Just as there is an abundance of irreconcilable Jesuses, the attempt to define religion leaves us in a forest of possibilities with no clear tracks. What sense does it make then to speak of religion at all? Why try?

The study of religion requires no *universal* definition. Instead

I want to propose a loose *working* definition that takes a cautious approach to the enigma. Start with the curious fact that when scholars discuss the so-called great religions—mainly Hinduism, Buddhism, Judaism, Christianity, and Islam—they overlook the fact that there is no institution, no human association of any kind, that approaches their *longevity*. Empires, nation-states, ideologies, families, even ethnic cultures can at best hold for a few centuries, but not for millennia. Roughly speaking, Hinduism is at least four thousand years old, Buddhism twenty-five hundred, Judaism more than two thousand, Christianity two thousand, Islam fourteen hundred, and none of them showing any clear signs of abating.

To be sure, all of these traditions have gone through significant changes from the time of their origin, but the key for us is that, most remarkably, each of them has been able to maintain its distinctive identity over great stretches of time. It is perfectly credible that, were it possible, a twentieth-century Aramaic-speaking Jew walking into Yohannan ben Zakkai's house of study in the second century CE would need no introduction to the discussion under way. A visit to the Mecca of Muhammad's time would show a number of architectural changes, but no modern hajji, or pilgrim, would feel the least out of place. Yogic disciplines in the Vedic age have varied little for three thousand years.

The term "identity" here is to be taken in its purest form. Lest we assume that these religions are at bottom all one, or at least variations on the same human impulse, we take note of the astonishing lack of influence of any of the five "great" religions on the others. Hinduism and Buddhism occupied the same space in northern India for many centuries. They borrowed extensively from each other in the arts and in mythology, and even spoke the same language. But there was never the least question for any of their members whether they were Buddhist or Hindu. Even where the Buddhists directly took over pictorial images of Hindu gods, they made a distinctly Buddhist use of them. No amount of exchange, in other words, compromised the essential identity of either. The same could be said for the way in which Jews, Christians, and Muslims shared the same territory, also for centuries, in the Middle East, and in Spain and North Africa. They knew one another's languages, studied their texts, frequently joined each other in dialogue. Yet never did Jews mistake themselves for Christians. No one was in doubt that there was an unbridgeable gap between them. Each religion, in other words, has an identity that sets it apart, so far apart that it cannot even be said that one religion is *like* another.

By "identity" I am not referring to some essence or even anything that can be shared. The identity of Islam is not some core *thing* that can be isolated from its context and be examined in the abstract. I am using the term in its purest Latin sense: *to have an identity is to be unlike anything else*. Islam, for example, cannot be understood in Christian terms, nor Christianity in Islamic terms. There is no category to which both belong. Personal identity has the same sense. I may be as human as you, but it is not our humanity that keeps me from being you. In spite of all that we have in common—and there is a great deal—you and I are radically distinct. I may think the same thoughts as you but I am not doing your thinking. There is for that reason no category that applies to both of us so far as we are genuinely ourselves and no one else. We have names, but the names do not define us; they only serve to indicate that I am not you or any other person. Hinduism and Judaism are in this sense names that function to prevent one from being confused with another.

Add to this another singular achievement: the creation of *communitas* that defies all boundaries of time and space. It is true that Jews in all ages and places are expected to read their primary texts—the Bible and the Talmud—in the original Hebrew and Aramaic, but it is also true that Judaism has thrived where Jews were native speakers of scores of other languages. Their immersion in widely diverse countries and cultures has not damaged or even substantially altered the unique identity of Judaism. Its *communitas* is of unbroken continuity. The same can be said for Islam. Although insisting that the Quran cannot be translated into any other language than Arabic, Islam has by no means restricted itself to the several countries in which Arabic is the native language, nor has it been captive to the culture of any one of the Arabic-speaking populations. Its identity remains unaffected by the vast range of societies in which Muslims have found themselves over the centuries. Hinduism, Christianity, and Buddhism have also never been diluted by any of the thousands of local customs and languages in which they have taken root. These are not loose associations of isolated individuals, but a unified people who have no other identity than that of their religion; they are not a culture, an ethnic population, a political unit, or a social caste. Buddhism is not a movement or a cult or an ideology; it is, well, Buddhism. It is not one of something else.

So we can at least say this about the existing religions: they have developed the genius of surviving, even thriving on, the challenges to their existence as a unified people over great reaches of time and space. What are we to make of this stunning phenomenon? No doubt believers, or members of those traditions, would have simple explanations: it is the work of the Holy Spirit, they might say, or it is Allah's guarantee that the faith of the first Muslims is the faith for all time, or it is that we have been numbered among the offspring of Abraham by God's promise to the Father of Faith himself. These explanations obviously come entirely from within each religion. They are therefore useless in addressing the claims of others. Are Buddhists children of Abraham, are Hindus beneficiaries of the Holy Spirit? Abandoning efforts to explain their genius at continuity from *within* any of the religions, can we find a way of speaking about its continuity that does not require us to say what religion *is*?

We can. The clue lies in the discussion of the multiplicity of Jesuses. As shown, Christians have reached very little consensus on who the "real" Jesus is, or was. At the same time, they cannot give up the quest. There is something about the man that is yet to be known, something unresolved, but something that *must* be resolved. For the same reason, the ceaseless yet fruitless attempts of Christians to develop an adequate description of their faith is a sign that its deepest and most compelling mysteries have so far eluded solution. To be sure, Christian history has been scarred by the rise and fall of belief systems devolving out of it, many of which have led to division, conflict, and even warfare. But then the belief systems repeatedly give way to fresh interpretations of both scripture and tradition—as the bellicosity of the Crusaders was replaced with the peaceful scholarship and service of the monasteries, as Protestants and Catholics have set aside their

RESERVED Date: 7-31-08

BOOKMOBILE *

Patron: Nick Nash

\#111115889

Phone: 269-1345

Title: Decent into chaos

Notified: 7-31-08

NA (WPU) LM: Person/ machine

Staff Initials: (AM)

Hold Until: _____

When calling a patron to come pick up a reserve or ILL say: "This is the_____branch of the library calling Ms./Mr._____. Your requested item is now available at the circulation desk. Please come in to pick up the item. It will be held at the desk for the next (3) business days.

7-31-08

Automobile *

Nick Nash
#111115089
2N4-1342

Descent into Chaos

brutal opposition in the recognition on both sides that neither is a closed system. This justifies the guarded conclusion that *it is ignorance and not belief that is the source of the faith's vitality.* What remains unsaid, even unthinkable, and what still inspires disagreement, is far more powerful than what is known and intelligible. If there is a strategy for preserving the unique identity of Christianity, it is not one that is planned in advance, as a battle or a campaign, but one that rises spontaneously from the acquired ignorance of its members. It is an ongoing expression of *communitas* that cannot be created by anything or anyone outside itself.

What is that ignorance *about?* This is the question we cannot answer except from within. It can take years of study for Christians, and non-Christians, to begin to have sufficient respect for what is not known about Jesus. As the Buddha was dying, his disciples asked him to name a successor. He named no one, saying that he was leaving them instead the sangha, the dharma, and the Buddha. The history of Buddhism is largely the attempt to ascertain what each of these three entails. What is the genuine Buddhist sangha, or community? What was the Buddha's teaching, or dharma? And who, after all, is the Buddha? After a lifetime spent meditating on and studying these questions one only begins to understand how elusive the answers are. Can we even imagine Muslims agreeing on what the Quran says? The point is that in each case, it is not a general ignorance but one that is acquired, one that is specific to each religion. We cannot say, therefore, what such ignorance is ignorant about. Buddhist ignorance is nothing like Jewish ignorance; neither is the least like that of Christians. This is why in each of the religions, ignorance must be *learned*. Recall that learned, or as I prefer to call it, "higher," ignorance is not ordinary ignorance (not knowing who will win the World Cup or whether there is a cure for cancer). Neither is it willful ignorance (refusing to acknowledge that we know we do not know). It is seeing that the desire for knowledge is ignited by what knowledge does not yet, and can never, contain.[45]

If we cannot say what Buddhists or Muslims are ignorant about, short of entering into the study and practice of their religions, we are nonetheless left with the fact of their longevity. *What* the religion is we cannot say; *that* it is and that it continues vigorously to exist, we must say. Of what use, then, is the word? What can justify our calling anything a religion? Nothing beyond *its longevity as a unified people*. First, thoughts about "longevity," then "unified people."

Longevity is, of course, a relative term. There is no obvious point at which it has been achieved. It is only a measure of the difference between the histories of separate human institutions. I have singled out the "great" religions because nothing equals their temporal range. There are, however, other traditions and institutions that have sustained themselves, in some cases, for centuries. The Roman Empire and ancient Egypt, for example, each had an enduring identity, one for seven hundred years, the other more than three thousand. The Norse, the Mongols, the Olmecs, the Navajos, and any number of so-called native cultures have all had long histories. We do not always refer to these as religions but their power of endurance deserves attention. Therefore, the term "longevity" cannot be used as a substitute for religion. I am not proposing it as the definition that has long defied scholars of religion. I am suggesting rather that we reserve the term *religion* for those institutions that have shown extraordinary powers of endurance. This provides some interesting uncertainties. It is easy enough to say that Sikhism is a religion while Fascism is not. Are Mormonism, Bahai, and Scientology on that basis to be considered genuine religions, as they claim, or simply aspirants? The question remains open; we will not know for centuries.

There is another category that belongs in the discussion: those that *claim* longevity. Both Marxism and Nazism saw their ideologies and institutions as timeless, already in possession of all the means necessary to endure for the full length of human history. Hitler spoke of the Third Reich lasting for ten thousand years. Marxism belongs to that family of political thought we can call end-of-history philosophies by claiming a vast longevity for themselves, while as we know now, Marxism itself, at least in its Soviet and Maoist applications, survived merely a few years into its calamitous and fatal history. For this reason, we can consider them "pseudo-religions."

In fact, both Nazism and Marxism have qualities that suggest they are belief systems that have evolved from Christianity. Hitler's "Reich" resembles nothing so much as Jesus's "kingdom of God" inasmuch as it is both now and yet to be and when fully realized will be eternal. Hitler's own messianic self-consciousness is undeniable. Marx's immovable laws of history sound strangely like the Christian believer's "salvation history," in which it is understood that absolutely nothing can rise to challenge God's final disposition of the universe, and thus its goal. What's more, Marx's vision of a perfect society in which "each gives according to his ability, and each receives according to his need" could be an alternate description of the final Christian community, possible only with the cosmic return of Jesus.

The world abounds in pseudo-religions: belief systems that declare for themselves an eternal validity but can show only modest longevity. The irony is that their demise is certain. They have few resources for responding to challenges from without or to changing conditions within. They have an absolute commitment to their own orthodoxy, something missing in all the great religions. Their boundaries are finally no protection against the inevitability that at least some of their believers will see beyond them and report what they have seen. For all of their apparent worldly power, therefore, they are surprisingly fragile even if in their brief histories they succeeded in inflicting considerable chaos and destruction on their designated nonbelievers.

It is important to keep in mind that the key to the meaningful use of the term "religion" is that it is to refer *only* to longevity. Whether the beliefs in question are true, or valid, or accurate, or verifiable, or questionable is irrelevant. Even that they are widely agreed upon adds nothing to their claimed authenticity. And by stressing longevity, we avoid claiming a religion's superiority by a count of the number of its members. That Christians outnumber Jews by a factor of hundreds has no bearing on the putative "success" of either. Also there can be no comparison on the basis of their beliefs, whether compatible or contradictory. Beliefs in God or in a classless society or in the endless rebirth of the soul are all neutral when weighed against one another. And whether they do or do not have priests, rituals, or developed theologies will not by itself earn the designation of religion. It follows that to apply the term "religion" to any human phenomenon does not necessarily have value implications; the oldest are not ipso facto the best. One might, of course, claim that great longevity adds positive value or validity, but this is not the claim I am making. As I see it, each of the existing religions, *regardless of its worth or its credibility*, has a genius at sustaining itself in the face of at least hostile and often horrifying opposition. It may seem a concept too thin for a substantive approach to a phenomenon as rich and complicated as religion. And yet the survival of *any* institution is a considerable achievement. One that survives over centuries can rightly be admired for its strategies. Those that stretch over millennia have obviously developed extraordinary resources for maintaining their identities. Even those of us who despise religion in all its forms must come to terms with the remarkable powers of renewal, especially among those religions that have outlived all other existing human associations.

It is here that we see the strongest difference between religion and belief systems. Belief systems offer a rational and consistent view of everything, whether it be how one should parent a child, what is to be taught in schools, or which enemies are most threatening. They also have a developed conception of history in which both the past and the future are unambiguously delineated. Religions are nothing of the kind. They are marbled with inconsistency, paradox, and contradiction. Rationality and truth seem to have no influence on the durability of a tradition. Its *communitas*, especially in its most vital expression, adheres to no particular pattern or ideology. There is no knowing in advance which track it will take. However learned one might be in the study of the gospels, nothing can be found in them that could presage the building of the Cathedral of Notre Dame, the founding of Oxford University, or the creation of the Holy Roman Empire. Participants in any given religion have only temporary consensus on the most pressing of issues. How one should parent is endlessly arguable. School curricula vary widely with no mandated core of subjects or methodologies. Whether a nation should go to war is a question that can never be satisfactorily resolved; even whether there should be a nation at all and, if so, what kind is a fitting topic of public dialogue. What religions do have is a pressing desire for talk: everything is fit for discussion, and though there is no guarantee on the outcome of the debate over key issues, each participant in it is prepared equally to talk and to listen. These conversations can become exceedingly rich and complicated, requiring long preparation for entering into them, and each of them is utterly unique. No one conversation is like another. To be sure, religion is not *only* conversation, but there can be no religion without a highly evolved skill of talk among its participants. And just as each conversation is unique, no one religion is like another.

The central argument of this book is that there is a *religious* case to be made against belief. Belief has been defined here as the place where we stop our thinking. When we speak of "defending" our beliefs, we obviously take them to be positions that we will hold against all challenges. The assumption is that we are certain about the truth of our beliefs, and that we are in hostile relation to nonbelievers. If there is a religious case to made against belief so defined we must clarify what is meant by "religious." Definitions of religion are famously difficult to make. Scholars have, in fact, largely abandoned the effort to do so. What *can* be said about the "great" religions is that there is no human institution that remotely equals their longevity, especially when we consider that they have also preserved their unity as a people who recognize themselves as a people. The heart of the collective life of these religions, or *communitas*, is unique to each. One religion cannot be understood in terms of another, or, for that matter, in terms of anything else. Their ongoing dynamism rises from the fact that they have not been able to clarify *for themselves* what their identity consists of. That is, they are animated by an ignorance that remains ignorance, regardless of the efforts to replace it with knowledge, or with belief. At its core, *communitas* is an active conversation concerning how it is to understand itself, and how it is to present itself to the world. This is in sharp contrast with belief systems that are an impediment to longevity—while paradoxically insisting on their own timelessness. They call for an end to change, except within carefully designated limits. They claim possession of certifiable verities. They remain willfully ignorant of the gaps and contrary evidence in their own histories. They assume that the future has collapsed back into the present, that nothing as yet unforeseen could prove their beliefs false. Such belief systems, in other words, are fittingly considered pseudo-religions, however intensely they declare their faith, however extensive their numerical expansion. And what is more, for all their claims of eternal validity, they have little endurance.

To have decided on the "real" Jesus, for example, is to assume that the quest to find him has been completed; there is no need to reexamine the events of the New Testament, nor to read through the libraries of works by those who have, nor to wonder what history has yet to uncover. Such claims are bound to expire, and quickly.

PART III

RELIGION
BEYOND
BELIEF

Communitas, though always unique to itself, exists nonetheless in the world. And its relation to the world is rich with subtlety and paradox. As noted, it is not *one of* any of the institutions or people or associations or organizations or political units or traditions that make up the world. It has no identity that the world can recognize. From the view of the world, it may be seen, incorrectly, as merely one institution among countless others. Members of the *communitas*—that is, the religious—know, however, that they are being falsely characterized when viewed that way. Their specific *communitas* is a stranger in the midst of the world even if the world does not see it as such. In Jesus's well-worn phrase, it is *in* the world but not of it. The challenge *communitas* faces in its relation to the world is to be at the same time authentically in the world without giving itself over entirely.

What is obviously implied here is that there is a clear distinction between religion and world. The distinction is a bit treacherous because it invites the old notion that the two are in essential conflict; the world on one side, and religion on the other. For believers this may be the case; for the religious such a dualism is not only meaningless, it is a path that leads to the Age of Faith II and eventually to the kind of havoc and chaos that abounded in the last century and threatens the present. Speaking of the relation of world to religion, then, I will simplify the discussion by using "world" to mean nothing more than *whatever communitas is not*. By such a definition, no valuation of either side is asserted.

Properly speaking, the world is not outside *communitas* or even around it. *Communitas* is unbounded in a way that belief systems are not. The world lies within its horizon; it is in the midst of the world. Just what makes up the world, from the perspective of the religious, is whatever they are able to see of it. But the horizon only marks the end of one's vision. If "the world," in Wittgenstein's famous remark, "is all that is the case," it is also all that *can* be the case, and that far exceeds the scope of anyone's knowledge. Because there is no telling what may yet be seen, the world will never fall completely within our field of vision. It is always more than can be seen. Thus, no definitive judgment about the world can be made. All knowledge of it is partial at best.

For belief systems, on the other hand, "world" has a completely different meaning. Inasmuch as believers hold their views in opposition to nonbelievers, they see themselves surrounded by hostile powers. When they look beyond their boundaries, they see only the boundaries of rival systems. They take their horizon not as the end of their vision but as the end of all that is the case. The world has nothing more to reveal of itself. Belief systems have already integrated all the revelation available. If there is any mystery there, it is only how the conflict will be played out. "World," therefore, is a decidedly negative category. When believers use the word "secular" (from the Latin word for world, *seculum*) or "worldly," it is a severe judgment on those whose beliefs are false, and dangerous. They are then in the world *and* of it.

The strangeness or alienation of religion in the world has other consequences. As long as it maintains its integrity, it cannot be used by anything or anyone outside itself; it is useful to no one. Rulers have in all ages and places attempted to cloak themselves in the timeless robes of the religious, or have otherwise appropriated the institutions and rituals of religion for their own benefit. For the same reason must the religions not use the world for purposes of their own. To the degree this happens, the religion is nothing more than a function of national or imperial polity. The temptation to rulers to exploit religion, and to believers to have the support of empire, can be extreme—because the benefits can be enormous. So-called faith-based initiatives implemented by the American government can ennoble its policies at a modest price, or at none at all, while the "faithful" can make use of governmental resources to subsidize their own initiatives. A far more dramatic example is Hitler's use of the German churches, Protestant and Catholic, to add to the pseudo-religious allure of his political agenda. The church's enthusiastic and patriotic response to its material support made it an effective tool for the state. With the swastika hanging in every church sanctuary, along with the cross, German Christians could easily conflate one with the other.

Because each *communitas* is a stranger in the world, it presents us with distinct limits to the generalizations we are able to make of it. What then can be said of any of the religions that falls short of assuming that we know what each of them is about? Because each *communitas* maintains its identity within the world, and not isolated from it, *we can view each of them as they have chosen to present themselves.* The view is necessarily external, but there is much we can say about where *communitas* and world meet, even if only from the perspective of the world. There are many ways we could approach it. I suggest we begin with its exuberant *orality*.

There is good reason to call its orality exuberant. In the opening verses of Genesis, God *said*, Let there be light, then the sea, the sky, the earth, and finally human beings. The Quran was *dictated* to Muhammad by the angel Gabriel. Muslims refer to it as a *recitation*. Immediately after his enlightenment, the Buddha *lectured* his companions on the fourfold truth. Having *read* the heavens, the Magi made their long journey to a *hearing* with King Herod to whom they *reported* what they learned. Angels then *announced* the birth of Jesus and Herod *decreed* the slaughter of all male infants. It was an angel who *delivered* the Book of Mormon to Joseph Smith. Angels in all traditions are *messengers*. Vanity of vanities, says the *Teacher* at the opening verse of Ecclesiastes; what follows is the sublimest *poetry*. A voice *called* to Isaiah out of the wilderness. Jesus *spoke* to thousands. Christians *proclaim* the gospel. They *confess* their faith. They *testify* to each other. They *evangelize* nonbelievers. They call their bible the Old and New *Testaments*. The word "gospel" means good *news*. The Buddhist sutras are *sayings*. The Upanishads are *teachings*. In the beginning was the *Word*, declares John the Evangelist. Disguised as his charioteer, Krishna *instructed* Prince Arjuna. Theologians *write*. Believers *proselytize*. The Pharisees *interpreted* scripture. The scriptures themselves, along with most all founding documents, developed from long *oral* traditions. The gospels were records of what the writers were *told*. John said there was no end to the *stories* told about Jesus. Jesus *blessed* the wine and bread. Judas *whispered* into the ear of a Roman soldier. Jesus *begged* God to spare him the suffering of the cross. Peter *betrayed* him three times. The crowd at his crucifixion *shouted*, Crucify him. "My God, my God, why hast thou forsaken me," was Jesus's *anguished plaint* from the cross. Paul said faith comes from *hearing*. *Midrash* is a unique literary style of the Talmud. The Mishnah was first a *verbal* collection of the ancient Jewish law. Abraham was *promised* a lineage that numbered as the stars in the heavens. Job *pleaded* with God to explain his suffering. God *answered* Job out of the whirlwind, *challenging* him to answer *questions* of God's own. *Voices* are heard in the wilderness. God *inscribed* the Ten Commandments on tablets of stone. Moses *raged* at his faithless followers. Liturgies are *chanted*. Prophets *prophesy*. Seeresses *foretell*. Oracles *pronounce*. The pope issues *edicts*. Mullahs issue *fatwas*. Adam *lied* to God in the Garden of Eden. The Psalms are *songs*. Jews, Christians, and Muslims are regularly *preached* to. Preachers *quote* sacred texts. Greek mortals *inveighed* against the caprice of the gods. God *warned* Lot's wife not to look back. Judith *flattered* Holofernes before beheading him. Buddhists have *auditions* with their teachers. Luther and other reformers came to be known as *Protestants*. Muslims *memorize* the Quran. Shamans *communicate* with the dead. The pope *excommunicates* apostates. Church councils publish *decretals*, *creeds*, and *articles of belief*. Errors of belief are corrected by *papal bulls*. Ecclesiastical law is known as the *canon*. Widely spread through the religions are such practices as *invoking* the divine presence, *reading* the entrails of animals, *soothsaying*, *conjuring* spirits, and *uttering anathemas*. When the gods or their agents appear, it is almost always with an outpouring of words: *consolations, commandments, reconciliation, promises, declarations, threats, condemnations, prophecies, judgment, reassurance, summons, orphic conundra, predictions, justification, maledictions, forgiveness*. Believers respond with an outpouring of their own: *prayer, confession, lamentation, thanksgiving, praise, blasphemy, pleading, speaking in tongues, protest, imprecation, repentance, speechlessness, intercession, excuses, promises, self-abasement, shouts of joy, expressions of awe and terror*.

In sum, religion comes to us on an oceanic flood of remarkably multiform linguistic phenomena. There are no institutions or societies that can claim even a modest equivalent. What are we to make of this? At a distance, all of this talk has a sameness, filling the quiet with sounds and the page with letters. Drawing closer, differences emerge. Predicting, summoning, singing, teaching, and praying are quite distinctive acts, difficult to place within a single phenomenon. And yet they have a connection that remains unclear until we look more carefully into the context in which they occur. But to find the connection, we need to know more about the specific religion that is their natural home. Chanting, for example, is an activity found almost everywhere, yet the content of the chant, its place in worship, and its effect on the chanter defy broad generalization. What do the intense rhythms and raised voices of Haitian voodoo have in common with the measured Gregorian harmonies of Christian monks? Does prayer serve the same function for Muslims as it does for Christians? So what appears at a distance as a smooth verbal mass becomes, as we approach it, highly textured and varied, an archipelago of coordinated linguistic acts separated by open and apparently bottomless waters.

And yet. By far the greater part of the world's millions are drawn to one or another of these islands. Remembering that each religion is an alien in the world, estranged from the usual categories of understanding, nevertheless the world finds them difficult to pass by, even if the attraction is hostile. Despite not being *of* the world, the religions have enormously prospered *in* it. The challenge to each religion is to reach out to the world without sounding like something familiar to the world, but also without speaking in a voice so odd as to find no audience. What then does draw the world into its discourse? It must be something more than the noise level of the chatter.

There are many ways of answering this question. From the point of view of the religions, some will declare that they were sent there, others that they accidentally arrived there, or that they were driven in by storms, or that they are returning inhabitants once lost but now found and coming home. But how does it look to us from off the coast? Why *do* people become religious? Here, too, theories abound. Well, they might be forced into it (via the severe rule of the mullahs?), or duped into it (by fraudulent evangelists?), or are victims of illogical thinking (by uneducated teachers?), or have simply landed in the midst of it by accidents of birth or geography.

I suggest another approach. Begin with the fact that the religions—or any *communitas* of considerable longevity—have grown up around mysteries of great depth and undeniability. It matters not what that mystery is, nor whether it is a mystery for anyone outside the *communitas*. Nor is it important whether the mystery is "real," or merely an invention or a phantasy. It is enough for us to acknowledge that, however the mysteries of the great religions are conceived, they have no equal in a *communitas* of ordinary duration. For example, although Americans have attempted for more than two centuries to argue through to a coherent statement of what America *is in itself*, it will take many more centuries of brilliant and original contributions to arrive at a sense of the unknowability of the American *communitas*—if it continues to exist—that even approaches the depth of the great religions. In other words, the longer the quest for answers continues, the greater the mysteries that inspire it. That is, the object of the quest becomes increasingly less intelligible even as the quest becomes more urgent.

Obviously, it cannot be ignorance alone that sustains the millennia of discussions. Just to be in the dark over what we are talking about does not by itself draw me in or, once in, keep me there. The long struggle to find the "real" Jesus does not continue just because he cannot be found. That what the Buddha meant by enlightenment has never been sufficiently described cannot be the only reason Buddhists have not stopped talking about it. Each of these vast discourses goes on because there is something at stake, something that *matters* to those engaged in it, that is critically important to them, something that they already find perplexing and in need of understanding, even if the understanding is only preliminary. We might say that we join the *communitas* when the questions being asked there become our questions.

This is all evident to us as we look on the religions as we draw closer. The extravagant wordiness of the great religions is most certainly not, as their critics love to characterize it, a collection of statements about the nature of the world. In fact, looking over the cited expressions, not a single one falls into that category. They repeatedly draw attention to what is *behind* the language, what cannot be said. Far from making claims of fact, they are in a variety of ways verbal responses to the unspeakable. They are more question than answer. They seem surrounded by a virtual penumbra of wonder. Moreover, there is an urgency in them: "Look now, do not hesitate, see where you are, change your life." If we are attracted, as millions are, *it is not out of agreement, since nothing is claimed, but out of a conjunction of questions.* We, too, are troubled and fascinated by unknowns of our own. Their answers, such as they appear to have any, are not as important to us as what we recognize as their need to find them. That need is something we share with them, not because we are religious, but because we are human. To be human at all is to live in an ill-lit zone of imponderables: Why am I alive at all? Where did I come from and where am I going? How am I to conduct my life in a world as confused as this? Why must so much of the world live in misery and violence? Why such collective self-destruction? Why do the evil prosper? Why is there something rather than nothing? To be sure, not everyone has such questions; they may wonder little if at all. They may be satisfied with what answers they have already found, or are certain they know how to find them, or do not care if they don't. Such persons—there are many—will feel no need at all to add their voices to this noisy crowd.

This provides us with the possibility of putting religion to a kind of test: find persistent and universal questions, common to our shared humanity, then, after exploring them briefly, see where the religions might come to meet them. The more impervious the question is to easy answers, the more it should reveal what occurs at the place where world and religion meet. It is difficult to see what is more puzzling and disturbing than the problem of *death*, and its companion, *evil*. Death and evil seem especially appropriate because in addition to their sheer persistence they are perplexities that believers are convinced they have solved. How, then, are they dealt with by religion, and by belief systems?

Inasmuch as the *communitas* is unique to itself, and therefore not definable in terms other than its own, it exists as a stranger in the world. The world does not know it as it is in itself. This does not mean that the *communitas* is necessarily in opposition to the world. It is in the midst of the world in the sense that its horizon falls within it. This means, because its members cannot see all of it, they know they do not have a comprehensive idea of the world, unlike belief systems. They accept the fact that there is much to learn there; the world for them is a bottomless reservoir of new information. As for the world, living for the most part within its boundaries, religion looks to them like any other worldly enterprise. If we look carefully at how the two meet, we see, from the world's perspective, that at the very least religion presents itself through an exuberant orality. Coming on a veritable flood of words, it might seem to the world from a distance that religion is just so much talk. A closer listening begins to reveal significant differences between the way these words are used by one *communitas* or another. They do not break down into a single mode of expression—thus the mistake that critics of religion make, assuming that all religious discourse is in a single mode—*descriptive*—and is therefore subject to rational and empirical analysis. In fact, essentially *none* of its discourse is descriptive. It is not making any claims about the nature of the world. And yet the world does listen. Why? One possible reason is that since the religious traditions grow up around inexhaustible mysteries, and since each of us by virtue of our humanity alone exists in an atmosphere of uncertainty, there is a possible conjunction of wonder at the point where religions meet the world. This suggests a kind of test: selecting deeply vexing questions that rise from our very humanity, we press them against the religions to see how they meet our worldliness at its most intimate expression. Although any can do, *evil* and *death* are questions that the religions must deal with to keep our interest and draw us into their deeper dialogue.

. . .

In one sense, death is the simplest of facts. Whatever lives will also die. Death is always paired with life. A stone cannot be said to have died, simply because it has never lived. Death is, moreover, a final event. To die is to come to an end without remainder. It is the absolute discontinuity of exactly that which had once lived. There is always the temptation to say that, well, *something* remains. It could be a soul, it could be an image borne in the memories of those who knew us, or it could be a transformed existence resulting from transmigration or union with a higher being. In each such case, however, we are not talking about death but the *survival* of death. There is something that does not die, a remainder of some kind. Obviously, when we shift to a belief in survival, however it is conceived, the issue of death disappears. It is no longer a question. It is absorbed into a belief system, where its hard factuality is joined to a larger continuity. But for those who find no relief from a belief system, the question of death persists, and demands to be answered in spite of its absolute imponderability.

Death is a fact, but what *kind* of fact is it? Because it seems to be so intimately connected to one's physical existence, the temptation is to view it in physiological terms and therefore an occurrence that can be objectively and empirically studied—as if death were something we could point to and *define*. What can be defined—although not without a shred of ambiguity—is the time of death. When is the body dead? When the heart stops? When brain waves go flat? When breathing ceases? Each of these has some usefulness for determining that final moment, though they can on occasion lead to considerable controversy. But even if we can agree on this matter, what death *is* eludes us. Scientifically, a great deal can be said, but science is concerned with continuities. As to what comes to a stop without remainder, or what begins without a discernible precedent, science must remain mute. Of course, there are physical causes and consequences so far as the body is concerned—one's genetic background, the act of conception, the decay of the flesh. None of this, however, can account for all that we associate with the birth and death of the persons we know and are.

Since it is a personal fact, the challenge is to see how close we can come to an understanding of our own death. Is it true, as Wittgenstein observed, that we can no more experience our own death than we can see the outer edge of our field of vision? Since the scientists are of no help there, perhaps if we turn in the opposite direction—to the poets—we will find a way of articulating the peculiar factuality of death, as an *experience of the end of experience*. But which poets? Each of us has our favorites, and no doubt most of them address the fact of death. But it would be difficult to find one who can direct our attention to the very moment of death more effectively than Emily Dickinson.

> I heard a Fly buzz—when I died—
> The Stillness in the Room
> Was like the Stillness in the Air—
> Between the Heaves of Storm—
>
> The Eyes around—had wrung them dry—
> And Breaths were gathering firm

For that last Onset—when the King
Be witnessed—in the Room—

I willed my Keepsakes—Signed away
What portion of me be
Assignable—and then it was
There interposed a Fly—

With Blue—uncertain—stumbling Buzz—
Between the light—and me—
And then the Windows failed—and then
I could not see to see—

In this case, the speaker in the poem has come as close as she can to the moment of death, while remaining just inside the terminus of experience. She is in her bedroom, surrounded by persons whose names and their relation to her are not disclosed. The room is airless. Those attending are silent and unmoving; their tears have dried; even their breathing has ceased. The poet has already bequeathed what she can; they will get nothing more from her. God is expected to make an appearance, but so far he is missing. The imminent death has already worked its effects. The attending guests seem lifeless, as if they themselves had died. The only obvious presence of life is the fly, wandering the room without knowing why or where ("uncertain" and "stumbling"). Except for the fly's buzz, there is only silence.

How did the fly get into this poem, even in its opening words? A vulgar and unwanted household pest, it has no place in the solemn and climactic moment ("that last Onset"). The fly is worse than vulgar. It is absurd, an animal that has no imaginable useful purpose, here or anywhere else, except to be an object of scorn and revulsion. Flies are to be killed and brushed away. But not this fly. Its intrusion seizes our attention, making us aware of the silence and lifelessness of all else. The fly reduces the weight of the moment, trivializes the great event.

The use of the fly has another effect: it displaces the common image of the winged soul leaving its bodily imprisonment for unbounded spaces, and in doing so it mocks the image. The fly, the poem makes clear, finds no opening for its escape. We imagine it tapping at the closed window, the only source of light in the room, unable to reach the light itself, and stupidly unaware of its confinement. The soul, too, is enclosed, windowed in, doomed to darkness. The soul, also like the fly, has no enduring substance. It has only one faculty: sight. The life of the poet, in whose voice the poem is written, consists now of nothing else. There is only consciousness, but in the famous last line of the poem, that also passes. There is no hint of immortality here. It is neither hoped for nor denied; it simply has no place in the poet's imagination. There is nothing left for her now except, like the fly, to be brushed away and forgotten—a process already begun by those attending and, apparently, by God as well.

In another of her so-called postmortem poems, "Because I could not stop for Death," Dickinson pictures newly dead believers, whom she calls "meek members of the Resurrection," enclosed in "Alabaster Chambers" where they have surrendered "Soundless as Dots—on a Disc of snow." A bleaker conclusion could scarcely be imagined.

Is it too bleak? To the believer, no doubt. What Dickinson has done for us here is to draw a vivid line between what can be known and what can only be believed. The phrase "members of the Resurrection" is ironic; by calling them "meek" we are reminded that however grandly we have represented death and our triumph over it, we are nonetheless reduced to nothing, as in the devastating phrase "Soundless as Dots—on a Disc of snow." Popular belief characteristically removes the irony. The members of the resurrection stay resurrected. They are now elsewhere. They live another life, yet grander than this.

The evidence, of course, is on Dickinson's side. Not only are our remains without substance, but we are soon forgotten. Both forms of the popular belief in immortality are rejected: that life continues in itself and in the lives of those it has touched. The tombs themselves are nothing more than "a Swelling in the Ground." Of life beyond the grave we haven't the least scrap of knowledge. What is more, the tears dry, we are quickly forgotten. Who grieves for the Civil War dead? Whose names belong to the stockpiled skulls of slaughtered Cambodians? What do we know of those who disappeared into remote Siberian labor camps? Even the individual victims of the Holocaust are slipping from the world's memory. The ebbing of this grief is itself a reason for grief. We are all but little more than the flies that Shakespeare has "wanton boys" idly kill.

If death as an absolute end seems too stark, consider its alternative: some form of immortality. Of course, not every form of immortality will do; it will be of no interest if it does not assure us that we can continue with our personal history and social context intact. If we cannot rejoin our family, or those whom we knew and loved, in a way that restores our original relationship, what is the point of continuing? (Gilbert Ryle, in his minor classic *The Concept of the Mind*, asked how much we would care if only our thumbs live on endlessly.)

The question of immortality is vividly addressed in classical Greek literature. (As for the Western understanding of the term, it can be argued that the question *derives* from the Greeks.) On the night before Socrates, condemned to death by a jury of five hundred Athenian citizens, was to take the fatal cup of hemlock, he was visited by a circle of his friends. Plato records the conversation that followed in his dialogue the *Phaedo* (although he does not name himself among those present). Socrates, in his usual dialectical style, argues that there is every indication that his soul will survive. And if it survives *as Socrates*, he will have the pleasure of challenging the philosophers who preceded him into death, to see if they were as wise as they thought they were. If he were not to survive, death would be as pleasant as dreamless sleep.

But not all Greeks regarded survival as such a pleasant prospect. The idea is challenged in the dark myth of the Sybil, or seeress. For transgressing against the gods, she has been condemned to everlasting life. On the face of it, the action seems like no punishment at all. However, in time, withered by the endless span of years, she can only squeak like an emaciated bird, begging for death. The Sybil's story provides a strong correction to Socrates' imagined life in death. His circumambulating the Parthenon and the Areopagus, engaging unsuspecting sophists reclining in the shadows, is a charming picture, but there is a naïve physicality about it, astonishing for someone of Socrates' immense intelligence. How many rounds could he make before he had exhausted all possible dialogue with them? From what we know of Socrates, once around will be enough to discover that they are not as wise as they thought. Then what? How could his endless existence differ from that of the Sybil? (Even in the popular, and understandable, notion that at death we will join lost loved ones, the question becomes what we could possibly *do* with each other over an infinite stretch of time that will avoid insufferable tiresomeness.) Immortality is a powerful fantasy, but on reflection an absurdity.

The notion that death is unreal, that we pass through the physical event changed, but as the same person, does not get much support from any of the great religions. In Hinduism, life is a plunge from pure and featureless being into a world scarred by needless suffering and willful ignorance. The oft-discussed belief in reincarnation is, contrary to mostly Western interpreters, not overcoming death so much as being ceaselessly fated to experience it. The goal of most Hindu spiritual disciplines is to find a way to step off the wheel of birth and rebirth, cleansing ourselves of any earthly particularity. Buddhism follows, but conceives the nature of the self differently: the self as we know it is a fiction created by our attachments to worldly objects. There is in fact nothing there, and therefore there is nothing to die. The Hebrew scriptures have the same stark view of death as Homeric literature. The self goes into a dusty limbo where it is soon forgotten and from which it can never return. Abraham is not promised by God to live forever, but to have no end of descendants, one generation after another, each dying but living under the same Abrahamic assurance of endless history. No immortality there.

Before we leave the Greeks, especially the Sybil's bitter fate and her antiphon in Plato's comforting hope for survival of the whole person, we should note that in the darker view of death there is a surprising insight into the way we experience life. For both the Sybil and Socrates, because they existed in an eternally repeated moment with neither past nor future, time itself disappears. Time, in other words, is a phenomenon available to us only by way of our mortality. Without time, experience is impossible; without experience, life is impossible. The fact is that we can have only one childhood. Old age is an experience that no child can remotely comprehend. For the aged, there is no return to that earlier time without viewing it from the years we are removed from it. Innocence once lost is forever lost. No experience is exactly like another. Even within an experience itself, time is steadily at work: it is never the same at the end as at the beginning, or even second by second. If our experience of life were to lose its temporality, its unrepeatability, we should soon tire of it, screeching to be relieved of its eternal boredom. The simple conclusion is that although we cannot experience our own death, *if there were no death there would be no experience.* The Greek philosopher Anaxagorus said that the gods' greatest gift is to conceal from us the time of our death. To that we can add that the gods' cruelest gift would be to deprive us of death altogether. The question of death, then, is inherent in the very fact of experience.

What do we find when the stark and pure fact of death comes to what I have described as the meeting place of world and religion? Remembering that I have proposed to view religion as that aspect of human institutions that constitutes their *longevity*, the question becomes, how could longevity be correlated with death? Indeed, is it not the case that many are attracted to religion precisely for its assurance that death can be overcome? We return to Dickinson.

Although she had grown up in the distinctly Protestant Christian community of Amherst, and although she was strongly urged to profess her faith during her first and only year of college, she remained an unbeliever. The language of her poetry shows the influence of her Christian environment, not only in its vocabulary but also in the way in which she has emulated popular hymns in the rhythm of her poems; many of them could actually be sung in measure with these tunes. Her rejection of prevailing belief is therefore all the more striking. Does this mean that she has departed from the Christian understanding of death to which she so lightly refers? Perhaps. But maybe it is she—and not believers—who has the profounder view of the religiousness of Christianity seen from outside its belief systems.

The trial and death of Jesus get extensive coverage in the gospel narratives; his death and resurrection are at the center of the New Testament as a whole. Do the scriptures offer an antidote that Dickinson misses? No, and yes. What is often overlooked is that in the gospel account Jesus dies a real death. The evangelists go to considerable graphic lengths to picture him as undergoing horrific torture, lifted down from the cross a corpse, stiff with rigor mortis, then wrapped for burial and entombed. Except for the presence of several speechless and grieving women, his friends have deserted him; he is as insignificant to the world around him as Dickinson's buzzing fly. It is a serious distortion of the text to assume that, like Socrates amiably drinking the chalice of hemlock among his companions, he will pass automatically to a preferred state of existence. As Plato reports it in the *Phaedo,* Socrates is in an equable mood, even joking with the prison guard who brings him the poison. Jesus, by contrast, facing imminent betrayal, arrest, and death in the Garden of Gethsemane, begged God to spare him the inevitable suffering. Even when an angel came to comfort him, his anguish did not cease. As he prayed, "his sweat became like great drops of blood falling on the ground" (Luke 22:44). The central event in all of Christianity is the resurrection that occurred three days later. But the habit of Christians to interpret the event as a guarantee of immortality has no basis in the New Testament. When Jesus was challenged by the Sadducees, a Jewish sect that explicitly denied immortality, to explain what happens in heaven, he answered, "God is not God of the dead but of the living" (Mark 12:27). True, he makes a great number of references to sinners cast into hell, as well as vague promises that he will never leave those who come to him, such as "Dwell in me as I dwell in you," frequently repeated with minor variations in the gospel of John. However, in his highly dramatic departure at the end of the gospels, he commands his disciples to repeat to the world what he has taught them, concluding only, "I am with you to the end of the age" (Matthew 28:20). There is nothing about meeting them in heaven or even that their deaths have been annulled. Without a labored tour through the text, it is still the case that altogether what Jesus said about the afterlife is subject to a very great range of interpretations. Paul, a literate Greek thinker, in contrast to the authors of the gospels, has the somewhat mystical notion that, once baptized into the faith, we are joined with Jesus in his death, thus "if we have been united with him in a death like his, we will certainly be united with him in a resurrection like his" (Romans 6:15). Still, it stretches the text to read this as a promise of immortality. Paul too is vague about the nature of the resurrected life. Altogether a consensus on the subject has never been reached. At best, we can say only that, based on the text, what happens at death and beyond is an act of God, as mysterious as everything else about God. In other words, we don't know. And we have no way of knowing. Dickinson's poem finds in the fact of death no hope for anything beyond it. The gospels find hope, but for what there is no saying.

There is another feature of Dickinson's poem that provides a clue into the religious approach to the phenomenon of death. Those who have gathered at the side of the deathbed are presented as so empty of life that it is they who seem already dead. They are nameless. They say nothing. Their relationship to the dying person is not mentioned, even to each other, as if now irrelevant. Nothing after this can hold them together. Whatever business has brought them to the room has been concluded. We can easily imagine them wandering off when the dying is finished, having nothing to say or to do with one another. That is, *there is not one death in the poem, but two*: first the poet, then the community of her friends. The contrast with Jesus's last appearance to his disciples is instructive: he made no promise to them that they will as individuals meet him in some timeless state. Although they are to disperse into the world, it will not be as the silent mourners of the poem, but as emissaries to report what they have been taught—whether by themselves or with others, it doesn't matter. What continues is not their souls, but the *communitas*.

We see this perhaps more clearly in the story of Abraham, who is not promised eternal life but descendants beyond number. As descendants, they are therefore all of one family. Here too it is the family, or *communitas*, not its members, that is deathless. However great or small the family may be, its continuity is the key—its continuity as *this* family and no other. No one chooses when or where to be born. In this case, the descendants are *chosen* as members of Abraham's lineage. And like families everywhere, they quarrel, betray each other, wander off—but their connection to the family is never dissolved. As if to emphasize this, the text immediately takes us through the anguished history of Abraham's relatives—his wife, his brother, his concubine, his sons, his grand-children, his great-grandchildren, and then on, never reaching a perfect society, but one that continues as the people of Israel.

It is a point of no small importance that Jews, Christians, and Muslims all regard themselves as "children of Abraham." He is commonly referred to as the "father of faith" in Jewish and Christian literature, and in Islam he is the second of the five great prophets—after Adam and ending with Muhammad—related by blood to each of them. We can only conclude from this that it is not the continuity of the immortal soul that matters but the con-tinuity of a people who regard themselves as members of the same body. It is a people who are united into a single family by a bond none of them can quite name though all of them engage in a centuries-long dialogue to do exactly that.

A feature of all the great religions is an emphasis on the singularity of a gathered people. We have already noted the importance of the sangha in Buddhism. Hinduism has wide recognition of bonds: blood families, castes, ashrams, followers of gifted teachers. For Muslims, the whole body of faith (umma) serves as the highest earthly authority. For Christians it is the church—in all its varieties and in all of its struggles with itself—that lives out the promise to Abraham as can no individual Christian, isolated from the ecclesia, or church (Gr. *Ek-klesia*: those "called out," that is, *chosen*, as are all of Abraham's children). Together they consider themselves brothers and sisters in Christ. If anything survives, that is, it can only be the *communitas*, and there can be no *communitas* except through the mortality of its members.

In most of the great religions, there is an emphasis on *lineages*. Hindus can name a long succession of masters who validate their immediate spiritual practices. Some Jews consider themselves descendants of the once prominent priestly class, others followers of a line of rabbis going back generations. Christians speak of "apostolic succession," a chain of authority that proceeds from Jesus's designation of Peter as the "rock" on which the church is founded—passed from leader to leader by a physical laying on of hands. In fact, the New Testament writers often are at pains to show that Jesus's lineage goes back to Abraham. Many Muslims claim direct descent from the martyred Ali, or even the Prophet himself. The significance of lineage is that "families" of faith are held together over great expanses of time, indicating both the permanence of their collective selves and the impermanence of its individual selves. The question of a person's life *after* death is of far less importance than a people's life *before* death as they continue their journey through the unpredictable turns of history.

Immortality, in other words, is a belief and makes sense only as it fits into comprehensive belief systems. It can fit into a broad variety of them. As Socrates framed the issue, deathlessness is of interest only if he could continue *as Socrates*. It is a conception of a changeless self, one untouched by the vagaries of time, even by the event of death. Socrates, that is, represents the notion of a fixed and unchanging reality that is inherently hostile to originality and demands the inerrant reduplication of its core beliefs.

For Nietzsche, "Platonism" was a metaphor for the mind-numbing, repetitive belief systems that have strangled Western culture from its origins. Christianity, of course, is his favored target, but philosophers and political theorists of all kinds are within his range. One can only imagine the spirited mockery with which he would have greeted the great and mad belief systems that followed his own descent into madness, especially Marxism and Nazism. What we learn from Nietzsche by his scornful treatment of what he calls Platonism (or sometimes "Egypticism") is that these systems acquire their power by way of denying death and the reality of history, even as they believe they have discovered its logic. Marx, following Hegel, described an eternal dialectic that accounted for all aspects of human affairs. Your place, and mine, in this scheme are already provided. We have a choice. We can embrace it and share in its eternality, or we can refuse to live by it, in which case we are as good as dead, thus making our arranged execution a mere bureaucratic nuisance. Of course, as these projects make their way through the mess of human history toward their perfect societies, some of the faithful will die, even many of them. But within the context of the ideology, they don't really die; they are assigned a kind of new life, promoted to the status of unforgotten heroes. Emphasizing the heroic is a necessary function of all belief systems. Nationalist movements abound in them. Some Muslims refer to their fallen warriors, their suicide bombers, even the innocent victims of war as martyrs, those whose deaths ennoble the struggle against their nonbelieving enemies. Every effort is made to create the illusion that the entombed Lenin appears to live on, and on. American veterans of World War II, offended by the oblivion to which they felt their nation consigned them, demanded that their sacrifices be enshrined at a location in the nation's capital prominent enough that they will be forever visible. In fact, it is impossible to find a public square anywhere that does not have a tribute to (un)forgotten heroes.

An important distinction enters here. For the most part, visitors to Lenin's tomb are not mourners, but something closer to compatriots. They do not come to grieve over his loss but to honor his continued presence in the Soviet pantheon, alive still in the potency of his ideas and the institutions that grew from them. Those for whom Lenin's ideas are dead or repellent would come to the tomb, if they come at all, with a different motivation—entertainment, perhaps, or sightseeing. The great majority of the monuments raised to national heroes serve to honor them in the same way. How frequent the comment that they have died that we might be free. Our freedom is celebrated as an honor to those who paid the highest price. Grief, on the other hand, is a recognition of the irrecoverable loss to us of those who died, and remain dead. Odd as it might seem, then, honoring the dead is a central ritual in belief systems; grieving for the dead, on the other hand, is a profoundly religious act.

A telling exception to the customary celebration of the hero is the Vietnam Veterans Memorial in Washington: a long black slab that resembles nothing so much as a fallen obelisk or an abandoned stele, one end already sinking into the earth as if it were doomed eventually to disappear, like Shelley's Ozymandius. The names carved into the stone seem to have been preserved for the ages, but they also have the dismissive anonymity of a telephone book, and are certain to be as forgotten as Ozymandius himself, "king of kings," along with his legions of heroic and victorious warriors. This is not a monument that honors the dead; it is a monument of grief, a reminder that death, however it comes, is still death.

Dickinson's poetry, though without doubt a work of genius, has a striking omission. Both poems cited earlier are thought to have been written within a year of each other, 1862 and 1863— that is, during the Civil War. She was not oblivious to the war. Indeed, she was enormously affected by the battlefield death of young Frasier Stearns, son of the president of Amherst College and a much-admired friend of the Dickinson family. Frequent references to the war and its horrors can be found scattered through her letters. But while scholars find intimations of it in her work, from a general reading of the poems we would not guess that the nation was engaged in a vast enterprise of killing, leaving more dead than all the other wars fought by the United States combined. Dickinson has few equals for her poetic treatment of death, but what is missing is an equivalent sense of the evil that lies behind the wider scope of human suffering.

History is often invoked to reassure us that the Civil War was a necessary, and therefore just, response to the evil of slavery. Slavery was certainly evil. It had to be brought to an end. But this does not cleanse the war-making of the North, any more than the South, of its own evil. The deep irony in this war, indeed in all wars, was that fighters on each side bravely risked death and ruin in the profound conviction that theirs was a work of stamping out evil. This was not a mere opinion, loosely held. It was a matter of deep and certain belief—on the part of both the Union and the Confederacy. The irony in the war is the irony in evil itself. No one is evil by choice, willingly and consciously, but only by the desire to eliminate it elsewhere. The burning of the Warsaw Ghetto was an event greatly celebrated as the deserved scourge of an offensive people; children danced in the streets, laughing at the burning bodies. They did not in the least see themselves as evildoers. The Serbs most certainly did not think of their brutal expulsion of Albanian Kosovars as a sign of their own evil; on the contrary, it was a heroic effort to claim land sacred to their own history. It was they, in fact, who coined the term "ethnic cleansing," suggesting that their ancient homeland was contaminated by the filth of intruders. In hindsight, it is astonishing how widely this was held even among educated Serbs, on the whole a highly civilized and talented people. What can we make of this except that evil finds its perfect home in our own belief system and the moral certainty that goes with it?

Evil is real. Just as death is real. The reality of both wrecks all attempts to hide them behind heroic, or poetic, or patriotic language. There is no denying evil, and no escaping it. Even if we engage in intense self-examination, even if we try to purify our intentions by extreme moral ardor, we are not free of it. The society of which we are consenting members, the nation to which we avow our allegiance and pay our taxes, the ethnic group or social class or political association we identify with—all of these to one degree or another have consequences that contradict our highest ethical motivation.

Just as no religious tradition can sidestep the intellectual and personal mystery of death, neither can it avoid directly addressing the reality of evil. In the Western religions, one of the greatest challenges to belief is the apparent contradiction in the morality of the divine will, summarized tersely in a chant from Archibald MacLeish's play *J. B.*: "If God is great, he is not good. / If God is good, he is not great." It is the problem known as theodicy—the attempt to reconcile an omnipotent God's goodness with the ubiquity of evil. Any number of books have been written on the subject of theodicy attempting to untangle the contradiction within God—unsuccessfully; the problem simply does not go away.

But to locate the problem within God is an error. The problem is human. It is what we do to one another that should be the focus of concern, not what God is doing or not doing to us. No matter how subtly it is attempted, there is no explaining away the genocidal ravages of the twentieth century. Evil is a crushing challenge to all believers, not just in the divine but in ourselves. No number of beliefs, and no passion by which they are held, can paper over the inherent uncertainties in our own morality. *The fact of evil is ultimately the undoing of all belief systems.* Because of their oppositional character, their attention is focused on the wrongs of the other. To admit their own wrongs is to draw into question the coherence of their beliefs and their trust in a chosen authority. To this day, there are millions of Russians who eschew all moral condemnation of Stalin's brutalities, considering them necessary to protect the integrity of the Soviet system. The protest of a great portion of the American population against the Vietnam War is still regarded by many as an offense against America itself. Because of the inevitability and universality of evil, genuine morality is the possession of no one. We can make no advance on Luther's observation that we are *simul justus et peccator.*

Can we then say what evil *is?* How shall it be defined? For believers the answer is simple: it is the organized opposition to their own believing community, an opposition of false believers who want nothing so much as the community's extinction. The Kosovars did not think they were being "cleansed" when their homes and their lives were destroyed, simply because their richly developed beliefs were odious to the Serbs. They were being "disappeared," to use the haunted term that describes so many evils of recent history. The Serbs, of course, thought their own historic belief system was being scorned, so how else to act but in defense of what they considered their genuine ethnic identity?

Still, giving examples is not a definition. Of definitions there are plenty. One of the most influential classical views was that of the Manicheans, who saw a cosmic split between good and evil. Though they were a popular sect of the ancient Mediterranean world, their teaching tenaciously survives even into the policies of American leaders. Augustine (once a Manichean himself) famously dissented, arguing that since all that exists has been created by God and that whatever he created must be good, evil can only be the absence of being, a teaching that had a long impact on Christian theology. What is missing in these definitions is the particularity of experienced evil. This is where the focus should lie, not on definitions but on the irreversible damage it does to human beings. Quite plainly, we know evil when we experience it or see it done to others. We know what evil is without giving it a cosmic meaning. In other words, if all we have are examples, examples are enough.

Where then does evil fit into our discussion of religion? From what has been said, it is obvious that religion offers no more a definition of, or solution to, the problem of evil than it does to death. But, religiously speaking, it is extremely important not to conflate the two. There is no question that death can be the result of an evil act. But it is also true that our mortality is a reality independent of evil. (To regard unintended death as evil throws us back into Manichean dualism.) If there were never anything terrible done to us, we would be just as fated to die. What must be remembered is that death is the possibility of experience. As with the Sybil, in the absence of death our voice is reduced to an unintelligible and unheard screech; life becomes endless repetition that is not life. Of course, death is properly to be lamented, grieved over, avoided wherever possible, and even raged at, but without it there would be no Shakespeare, no Buddha, neither beauty nor wonder nor even words.

The experience of evil, by contrast, is not the experience of silence but of being silenced, whether by death, injury, isolation, deprivation, mind-numbing ideology, the designed crushing of one's culture, or something as common and simple as not being listened to. Though Abraham was promised an endless succession of descendants, there is no counting the attempts, and the variety of attempts, to thwart the promise, to bring this grand and open-ended journey to a conclusion, to silence the Jews altogether. Extinguishing millions in the pre-Columbian Americas along with their languages, their cultures, their arts; the Japanese forcing the Koreans to speak only Japanese, even to change their names accordingly—the chronicle has no beginning and no end.

Whereas death is a condition or state, evil is always a human act, undertaken freely. It is important to stress its voluntary character because if an evil act has a preceding cause, then it is not evil but the outcome of a natural process quite as inevitable as death, rendering its human agent helpless to resist and not culpable for what is done. If murderers are described as those whose childhood was so deranged, their lives so unsettled, that they were driven to the act, then they are not murderers but victims of social and physical circumstances—which themselves have causes. Equally, if the murder is pictured as a cosmic force, a satanically driven act, it is the devil's work and not the murderer's. This is absurd, of course, for it is an insult to one's humanity, denying us our essential freedom, implying that we are automatons none of whose actions are properly thought to be our own. If this were so, we would be as incapable of good as of evil. (Some circumstances, however, can be so destructive to a person's freedom and rationality that it is appropriate to modify a judgment against them; though what they do may be evil, they are nonetheless victims of evil themselves.)

One of the most indispensable effects of religion is to turn the ascription of evil back on ourselves. "Why do you see the speck in your neighbor's eye," Jesus said, "but do not notice the log in your own?" (Matthew 7:3). The teaching is hard, for even when evil is plainly done to us or to others, the religious reaction is not first to hold evildoers responsible but to search for the evil that is ingredient in our own reaction; if we do accuse them we do so as persons equally capable of evil. In fact, never can we make a judgment of another with clean motives—even when such a judgment is appropriate. Evil is real. It is unmistakably there in the world, and just as unmistakably in ourselves.

This brings us to an ironic conclusion: because evil so often rises from the attempt to eliminate it, *doing good is not the opposite of doing evil*. This is not to say that the good should not be done, nor that good is often done. It is rather that in each effort to alter the deeds or the circumstances of others so much remains unknown and unpredictable that there is no certainty that our own actions will make the lives of others better or worse. Even when we see most clearly what needs to be done, we must be extremely careful not to look around the log in our own eye. Any conception of what the good is must be tempered by a personal fallibility beyond erasure; that is, by a horizon's ignorance.

. . .

We began this section by applying a kind of test to the religious response to the most troubling of human questions—death and evil. The finality of death has been difficult to accept. If there is something remaining after the event of dying, it is not truly death. The stark reality of death fascinated the Greeks, seen in Socrates' equable attitude toward the likelihood of immortality, in which it is the full personality and its social context that survives. The contrary view, as in the story of the Sybil, is that deathlessness can only be the utter destruction of anything resembling human existence. Our very humanity, therefore, is only possible because of the ultimate finality of our personal being. Death is a fact, but what kind of fact? Science, dealing only with continuities, has nothing to tell us. Turning to the poets— in this case, Emily Dickinson—death is seen first as a separation from others; it is not only we but our relationships that die. Dickinson mocks the notion of the soul as something that might escape this kind of death. She also mocks the notion of the resurrection, at least as it is popularly represented in Christian thought. In other words, Dickinson presents the question as strongly as it can be stated. What is the religious response? The religions, contrary to the common notion, take death as a reality; their view is more like that of the Sybil than that of Socrates. Socrates' comforting assurance of *immortality* is much more a property of belief systems. Since ideologies presuppose that all substantial change has been erased, even the existence of its individual members has its permanent place, as we can see in the widespread monumentalizing of its heroes. And as for *resurrec-*

tion? Much is said of its promise in the New Testament, but to assemble it all into a coherent view has eluded us for two millennia. The prevailing biblical view of death is more evident in the story of Abraham, who was promised not eternal life but an unending succession of descendants. That is, it is not the individual self who survives but the *communitas* in which the mortal self has had its life. What Dickinson overlooks in her discussion of death is its dark cousin, evil. It is important to distinguish the two. Death is a state, evil an act. Death can, and often does, result from evil acts, but it is a mistake to conflate them. Evil, like death, is an irreducible reality, but it comes with a disturbing irony: evil is nearly always an attempt to eliminate evil, as it appears in those who oppose us. It therefore thrives in belief systems inasmuch as it is easily ascribed to their enemies, the result being a spiraling expansion of evil. As for the religious, there is a consistent demand that wherever we see evil, we see it in ourselves as well. Whereas for belief systems the future is closed, for the *communitas* everything is done to keep it open.

I have proposed that we approach religion by observing how it approaches us—through its extraordinary orality. In what equivalent way do belief systems approach us? It must first be acknowledged that belief systems are enormously adept at drawing the world to themselves. They too come at us with questions. Where effective, they directly challenge whatever it is that we do or think. Are we being exploited by the rich, or are we unfairly taxed to support the poor? Do we really know when the fetus has attained true personhood, or are we supporting the murder of the innocent unborn? Are schools teaching our children to be soundly patriotic, or to be bitterly critical of our national priorities? What in fact are we worshiping in our churches and temples, a genuinely biblical god or an abstraction drawn up by indifferent scholars? These are all genuine questions and deserve to be answered. If the religions generally answer them only by adding to their imponderability, it makes sense that we would be attracted to the convincing solutions belief systems provide. Their great advantage is that they fairly bristle with answers, leaving no ambiguity in their declarations of truth.

But as we have observed, truths so provided are targeted at mirrored falsehoods. They are essentially dyadic. Every offered belief has its distinctly objectionable opposite. The world has been neatly divided. For that reason, questions, even when genuinely asked, seem to be little more than triggers for answers already prepared. Whatever they declare is matched by what is to be denounced. One of the results is that the questions cannot be turned back on those who have composed the answers. Belief has been thoroughly washed, cleansed of its uncertainties. Believers have little to learn from the world. Its basic issues have already been resolved. But the world itself, of course, lives largely in error. Therefore, there is no need to *listen* to the world, but every reason to *speak* to it.

To be sure, believers may in fact listen to the voices of the unwashed, but they do so only for reasons of rebuttal. Creationists and advocates of intelligent design study the despised work of evolutionary scientists not to listen to what the scientists say but to find lacunae through which they can insinuate their own theories. Sometimes rebuttals may seem to take the form of careful, drawn-out rational arguments (as in Aquinas's monumental *Summa Contra Gentiles*, or John Henry Cardinal Newman's masterful *Apologia pro Vita Sua*) that attempt to find common ground between belief and unbelief that will then assist unbelievers in crossing over to "our side." Still, the line remains unambiguously drawn, as indicated in the term "conversion," or "turning" away from falsehood to the truth. Settling for the common ground is not an acceptable substitute for belief. The strategy has little elasticity. It is an effort to convince others to stop thinking their errant thoughts.

"Dialogue," therefore is obviously not the correct term to describe the way belief systems address the world. Other terms quickly suggest themselves: *broadcasting*, for example, or *airing*, or *loudspeaking*. A broadcaster is determined to attract the largest possible audience for what has already been written or scripted, essentially foreclosing any possibility of exchange between speaker and audience. The broadcaster is often removed by distance or time. Airing can be thought of as a milder form of address. The prepared language is made public and listeners are encouraged to take on the thinking of the speaker, but are essentially expected to work it out on their own. Loudspeaking is another matter. Although the "message" may be the same, its delivery is more aggressive. A loudspeaker has the quality of blanking out anything else that might be said, to the point of silencing the listener's own thoughts and replacing them with the language and sentiment of the speaker. It has been reported that at the military prison in Guantánamo, Cuba, the national anthem was played at high volume just when the Muslim captives attempted to make their call to prayer. We are also familiar with the phenomenon in such places as North Korea, where Kim Jong Il's face and voice are everywhere, even in radios installed within each home, and in a milder form, Syria, where Bashar al-Assad's image is on billboards, stamps, and in nearly every shop window. "Here I am," these strategies say, "think of no one and nothing else." It is a kind of loudspeaking raised to such a level that it blanks out the very thinking of those who fall within its range.

Broadcasting, airing, and loudspeaking are modes of address between believer and unbeliever, but also among believers. Once believers have selected their authority, genuine dialogue is abandoned. Discourse does not take its own spontaneous path but is aimed always at correcting and strengthening the existing thinking of those who already believe. Indeed, an attempt at genuine dialogue within the belief system can be taken itself as an act of unbelief. Government employees, especially those in the military, may have their own thoughts on a great many issues, but to challenge orthodox policy can quickly end or damage their careers. To remain on the "inside," they forgo open dialogue with their superiors; officially, they must be considered true believers. If a priest in the Catholic Church were to call for a complete reexamination of celibacy in the clergy, he is certain to be silenced in one way or another, from being ignored to being defrocked.

There are two kinds of authority, one common to belief systems (power) and one to the religions (poetry). When believers broadcast their truths to the world, it is obvious that they are simply quoting from an existing statement of them. They have a final authority, usually a *text*, or if not a text as such, teachers or institutions that have the same role as a definitive text. It is obvious also that religions have texts of their own. Their extravagant wordiness emerges from a series of authoritative works, or figures, but the ways their texts are used could not be more unlike those of believers. Since there is widespread confusion about the role of texts (critics love to quote them as though their use is uniform and restricted to their literal surfaces), it is essential that the differences should be indicated.

Critics are correct in their reading of texts "literally" insofar as some believers read them the same way. What they regularly fail to see is that the *religious* use of texts—whether sacred scriptures, founding documents, or the dominant voices of the *communitas*—departs radically from such literalism. They do not rise straight from the page to the mind. Their primary importance is not to offer up truth and falsehood, but to urge readers and listeners to an active inquiry into what is true and what is false. They must be *interpreted*. That is, they do not come to life until there is a living response to them. It is as if they create a silence around themselves that cannot remain a silence but demands original words from the listener.

For its place in this discussion, the word "interpretation" can be taken in its simplest form: speaking or writing about a text in terms other than those that occur in it, and doing so to affect the way others read the same text. I offered an interpretation of Dickinson's poem not by repeating exactly what she had written, but by a number or words and sentences not found in it. There are two questions this definition immediately raises: (1) Will *any* words (or actions) do for an interpretation? (2) *What* exactly is being interpreted? As for the first question, why are my comments any different from a random series of remarks that have nothing directly to do with the poem itself? There is no doubt that other readers would have said something very different in response to it. As I use the term here, an attempted interpretation becomes one only when it leads others to comment on or think about the poem; that is, only when it expands the discursive context in which the poem is a fitting subject. For that reason, there is a very wide range of reactions that could qualify as interpretations. Counting up its syllables, describing its meter, entering into the possible psychology of those present—all of this and many others qualify if they succeed in expanding the discursive context. Many attempts at interpretation—including mine—will fail to be considered such if they do not meet this criterion. The second question—what exactly is being interpreted—is a subtler issue. Is there something *there* to which our words can attach themselves? Does the poem (or the sacred text) exist as an entity in itself, offering substantive ground for what we are talking about? The subtlety of the question derives from the fact that the poem itself is an interpretation. An interpretation of what? we might ask, and turn to that which it seems to interpret. But that too is an interpretation, and so on indefinitely. Does that mean we are talking about *nothing*? The answer to this question lies at the very heart of the thesis of this book: we are talking about the poem only when it has been taken as such by those whom we are addressing. In other words, the answer to both questions points to the setting in which the conversation continues. In the case of Dickinson, the setting is composed of many thousands of readers, scholars, and artists—all engaged with each other in a conversation that has a unifying center. What that center is cannot be said, for as we noted, once all the participants agree on what they are talking about, the discussion ends. In other words, the critical world surrounding Dickinson is a *communitas* whose forms of thought, modes of address, styles of engagement, and guiding concepts are unique to it. Anyone is free to enter this body, but their membership depends on the degree to which they are able to find hearers among the others. The interpretation of religious phenomena has the same character. Many biblical interpreters, for example, seem to be searching for the "text behind the text," or what the Bible is "really saying." This suggests a ghost document, out of sight of the regular reader, but one that can be found by the proper approach. Why, however, should that ghost text not have a ghost of its own? Being able to interpret Buddhism or Stoicism or Islam "properly" does not require us to get at the very essence of each but to succeed in taking our place in the discursive contexts surrounding them.

In discussing the way the world is attracted to religion, I propose that we think of the place of meeting as a *conjunction of questions*. We give our attention to the discourse of a given *communitas* when we hear in it echoes of our own doubts and wonders. For that reason, genuinely religious language has a broad *resonance*; we hear in it a re-sounding that gives religious texts their particular power or beauty. To offer a homely illustration, dropping a stone into a pool of water and discovering it is but an inch or two deep is markedly different from dropping it into a sea immeasurably deep; it is a difference of sound, the one an annoying slap, the other a profound (from the Latin *profundus*, or depth, as of the oceans) boom, indicating there is much beneath the surface, as yet unseen. The creation myths in the opening verses of the book of Genesis, for example, are particularly resonant, having echoes in the language and the thinking of Sumerians and Babylonians—civilizations that had vanished a thousand years earlier.

The noisy quarreling over the "theory" of creation regularly overlooks the fact that in the very first words of the book of Genesis, from which the putative theory of believers is drawn, there are not one but two stories of the beginning, stories that flatly contradict each other, and have been composed by different writers whose own texts show an original interpretation of earlier texts. To make the matter even more curious, one of them—by the so-called Priestly writer—has pronounced echoes of Babylonian myths that themselves echo earlier stories going back several thousand years before Genesis was composed. The core of these stories is the act of the god Marduk splitting open his mother Tiamat by a violent wind creating the sky above and the earth below—as the earth is separated from the heavens in the Priestly account. There are striking narrative and verbal elements obviously influenced by these ancient tales. What is more, the text of these opening verses of Genesis have the self-evident character of poetry or even of liturgical songs, chanted or sung in worship ceremonies. To suppose that they offer a "theory" of creation, of the same sort Darwin proposed, is a grave misreading of the text, omitting its great historical, linguistic, poetic, and liturgical depth. Making a protoscientific treatise of this song, thus depriving it of its grand resonance, suggests that a "literalist" reading of the Bible is not reading the Bible at all.

For another example, when John opens his gospel with the

profoundly elegant "In the beginning was the Word" (Gr. *ho logos*), he calls up a long history of the Word's use. "Logos" has played extensively into ancient discourse on such matters as the nature of mind, the structure of the universe, a coherent process of thought, and the ideal order of society. John himself joined a discussion that had centuries behind it. It is likely, of course, that he was drawn to the expression for its ineffability; he may not, that is, have known exactly what he was saying. By evoking this history, he has joined these voices not as a corrective or a final resolution of the meaning of the Word, but as a member of a chorus of many singers. What the Word finally means he leaves to its rich choral expression. As in a musical ensemble, if all the instruments were identical and playing the same tune, we would be soon bored and turn elsewhere. Instead of the harmonic interplay of many voices magically conjoined, there would be little more than noise.

In fact, nearly every event in the life of Jesus is strongly reminiscent of a host of mythic tales from a wide variety of sources. Begin with the fact that his birth was announced by mysterious astrologers from the East—as if he were already known in distant regions. The birth of heroes is regularly announced by such figures or by angels, quite as angels appeared both to Mary and Joseph. Their parentage is always confused. Jesus is both the son of his earthly parents and the Son of God. Because heroes are always the sons of kings or nobles or gods, whose birth is a threat to the father's rule, the fathers go to lengths to see that the child will perish. King Herod's slaughter of the infants was an attempt to protect himself from the new "king." The threatened king may expose the child to brutal elements, as Oedipus was left in the wilderness, as Moses was sent to float on the Nile, as Jesus and his parents were forced to take flight across the desert to Egypt, echoing the "exposure" of the child hero. The infant is often born in distressed natural settings, frequently in association with animals, as Jesus in the manger surrounded by animals, as Romulus and Remus nursed by a she-wolf and fed by a wood-pecker. The parentage of heroes is often in doubt, the hero be-lieving his real father was the voluntary substitute who was raising him in humble circumstances—as Joseph is not really the father of Jesus, as the shepherd was not the father of Cyrus, as the pharaoh was not the father of Moses. Virgin birth is common. When the king of Argos was warned that his daughter, Danaë, would bear a son; he locked her into a tower, but her child, Perseus, conceived by Zeus in the form of a shower of gold was born half human and half god. Even the Buddha, according to a dream of his mother's, was divinely conceived not by his worldly father but by a mysterious white elephant who had entered her palace unseen. The young hero inevitably fulfills the prediction that he will displace his father. Laius was warned that his son Oedipus would kill him and marry his wife, Jocasta, and so it happened. Mythically speaking, Jesus takes the place of his father as the ruling lord, and Mary, though perfectly human, would in time be elevated to divine status, where she would rule with her son as the Queen of Heaven. The richly detailed story of Jesus's death is shaded throughout with mythic themes and events. He is betrayed by one close to him, as heroes everywhere. His death on the cross, or tree, which precedes his resurrection and new life, is reflective of the Tree of Life in the Garden of Eden; the Bodhi tree under which the Buddha was born; the tree at the center of the world, "Yggdrasil" in Norse mythology; the great post that supported Isis's palace and discovered by her to contain the body of her lover, Osiris, whom she later resurrects. Above all, it is necessary for the hero to die a painful death, but a death that has redemptive and restorative powers for those whom he gave his life to protect. These resemblances spread outward into all known cultures and religions, a full accounting of which could not be contained in a single volume.[1]

It is not accidental that the two most common instruments for religious expression are the bell and the drum, each a marvel of resonance. A bell, like a drum, if properly designed and constructed has extraordinarily complex patterns of sounds that play off one another. Because their internal echoing continues even after we cease hearing it, they suggest a vitality that far exceeds our awareness. Bells seize our attention at once. Until relatively recent times, they were the means of alerting citizens to such varied phenomena as fires, enemy attacks, the time of day, transitions in ceremonies of worship. Buddhist monks and nuns beat a skin drum or a wooden bell to focus the mind. The volume of a bell's sound is of less importance than its clarity. Drums played in rhythm can lead listeners to ecstasy and frenzy, whether in religious ritual or rock concerts. It is more than symbolic that for centuries European armies melted down church bells to be recast as cannons, as if the goal was not to reach listeners but to deafen them.

One characteristic of music well played is that the listener is effectively drawn into it. This might mean actually joining in with instruments of our own, or a transfixed listening that reaches deeper than any word or instrument can possibility penetrate. In fact, we do not hear the sounds as music until we are drawn into them. And when we are, there is in the expression of the whole something far greater than any of its parts, which cannot be expressed except through the music. Nothing can be said about a symphonic performance that exceeds the performance itself. The same is true of poetry or dance, or any other work of art, verbal or material. In attempting to say who Jesus is, the best we can do is to utter words provoked by the collective attempts to do so over the centuries—a choral work we cannot possibly translate back into a few phrases, any more than we can assume that a concert is adequately described by its listing in the program, or that a painting is interchangeable with its title. Reading the program or the museum's catalogue, we have no notion of what actually was performed or displayed. We can extend the metaphor: a literal reading of the Bible amounts to little more than what we learn from a concert program, or even the score. It is the symphonic whole that bears the meaning that nothing less can remotely capture.

What makes religion's exuberant orality religious is using it to enlarge our own expressive capacities. It is learning to dance to the words or to sing with them or to refashion them into original creations that capture what we experience as the mystery within them. This is why the great religions come to us not only in their words but in a culture that embraces every form of interpretation. We cannot see Jesus except through the cathedral at Chartres, Russian iconography, Bach's Mass in B Minor, and the poetry of Gerard Manley Hopkins. Nor can we see Muhammad except through the Dome of the Rock, Sufi dancers, and the names of the stars. True, the outer edges of this culture seem as worldly as they are religious. Buddhist temples are stunning works of art even to someone without the least understanding of the *communitas* that produced them. Christians founded the first American universities as an expression of faith; that they are also great centers of secular learning is no contradiction but a demonstration of the harmonic meeting of world and religion. These cultures have taken many centuries to develop. They are the creation of no single person, or institution, but of an evolving imaginative response to the ineffable. (It is true that St. Peter's Cathedral in Rome would not have existed as it does without Michelangelo; but it is also true that without the long spiritual tradition preceding him, there would have been no Michelangelo.) This is what prevents us from applying the term "religion" to shorter-lived phenomena, such as Mormonism. It has not yet developed a distinctive culture of its own; there is no music, or architecture, or philosophy, or even theology, that is recognizable as a unique expression of the Mormon faith. So far, at least, its cultural imagination has apparently not grown much beyond its program notes. In spite of the wishes of some to conceive of America as a religious nation, there is far too little culture that is exclusively American to merit the claim. Its culture is extensive, but overlaps so broadly with others that it is difficult to isolate any large part of it as truly American. Insisting on its religious, or more often Christian, origins is more the attempt to translate "Americanism" into a belief system than into a genuine religion.

What is more, because religion requires centuries to grow an extensive culture around itself, it is all but impossible to *invent* a religion, as if it were an achievement of Joseph Smith or the founding fathers. Jesus is not, as he is sometimes described, the founder of Christianity. Not only was Christianity a much later development, it is doubtful he even knew the word "Christ." Even though the evangelists were writing in the context of a (still primitive) Christian institution, they ascribed to Jesus no talk about a community that has any resemblance to the church as it came to be. It is even too much to say that Christianity was the creation of Paul, or even of all the New Testament writers combined. The development of the church was not planned, not conceived in advance, but followed a path determined as much by the world around it as by its own faith. Neither Paul nor the evangelists could have predicted what was to come—even though its identity as a *communitas* remained fully intact. Indeed, we can reverse the founding act. It is not Jesus who created the church but the centuries of quarreling and searching Christians who invented Jesus.

Mystics of the early Middle Ages, especially Jewish mystics, came to an observation about the nature of religious language that contributes handsomely to our understanding of its peculiar appeal. As they interpreted difficult texts like the nearly unintelligible Zohar, not to mention any number of puzzling biblical passages, they noted that the meaning of the words lies not in the darkened part of the page but in the white spaces surrounding them. Correspondingly, in spoken language the meaning is not in the sound but in the silence out of which the words emerge and into which they return. As for the written word, the point can be simply made: if the spaces were blackened with ink, the page would be illegible. There would be nothing there to read. If the page were unmarked, by the same reasoning, nothing would be said. On the other hand, if what *is* read is *only* the sentence as it is inscribed, its meaning can consist of nothing more than a repetition of itself. Consider a biblical example: God placed the serpent in the Garden of Eden. What could that possibly mean? Reading only the darkened lines, the answer can only be: God placed the serpent in the Garden of Eden. We have gone nowhere with it. If the meaning of the Zohar is the Zohar, the book would be worthless. Moreover, language itself would be worthless; we would cease writing and speaking, and thinking.

If we allow the spaces back into the biblical comment about what God did with the serpent, then its meaning can only be a different comment. But how are we to know exactly which comment this should be? If we consult the spaces, we will of course learn nothing. No rule of interpretation appears in them. Indeed, any rule will have its own spaces, making an explicit repetition of it useless; thus the rule too will have to be interpreted.[2] What shall we learn from this except that there is within and around each word and each sentence and each book no end to possible interpretations? What is more, there is no right or wrong reading of any human expression. Moreover, there is nothing particularly rational in these extended dialogues. They explain nothing. Their power lies chiefly in the interpreter's skill at provocation.

It follows, then, that the potency of a sacred text—the very thing that makes it a sacred text—is the dynamic it creates between the printed word and the white spaces surrounding it, or between the spoken word and the silences that follow. This is why they are texts that *demand* interpretation, but without any indication of what that interpretation should be. The Bible, for example, provides no guide to reading the Bible. In fact, it is full of such inconsistencies, contradictions, lacunae, obscurities, baffling tales, and poetic imagery that to quote it at all is to select from conflicting alternative passages. Every quotation is therefore necessarily an interpretation. For this reason, a "literal" reading of the Bible is not a reading at all but an arbitrary choice of one passage over another, and a putting it to use of saying what the reader has already decided it should say (although that is also an interpretation, merely unrecognized as one by the reader).

In sum, what belief systems conspicuously lack is music. They are monotonal. One voice speaks for all others. If it varies, it is only in amplification. Resonance between believers and the world is replaced with repetition. The stone hits the pool with a thin slap; however wide the pool of believers, we find that it is only an inch or two in depth.

CONCLUSION: FOR THE
RECOVERY OF WONDER

In light of the impossibility of finding a universal definition of
religion, I propose using the phenomenon of longevity as a way
of arraying human associations, reserving the term "religion"
for those at the farthest end of the time scale. Critical to the use
of this standard is that the association in question must maintain
its identity throughout—that is, its identity as *communitas*, and
not just as a political entity, or *civitas*. These terms are not precise and apply only to broad reaches of time, with a great variety of forms. There are, of course, many possible expressions of
communitas, and not all of them are religious. In fact, very few
of them are. *Communitas* can appear and disappear in moments.
Neighborhoods, clubs, schools, athletic teams, families, artists'
leagues, military platoons, workplaces, professional associations,
environmental organizations, churches and temples, garden
groups, choirs, political think tanks, even corporations—there is
almost no gathering of human beings that does not have some degree of spontaneous culture that holds it together around a shared

interest. But families disperse and die out; without sufficient hostility ethnic identities fade away (the Irish in America); armies lose their enemies and thus their most intimate bond (veterans of the Vietnam War); corporations divide, workers retire or are fired. Even churches trade away vast treasuries of biblical and theological thought for passing issues of contemporary ideology (Episcopalians dividing over the place of homosexuality in their polity).

At what point then can we judge that *communitas* has existed long enough that it can be properly called religious? Counting the years, or the centuries, is not enough by itself. The more delicate judgment has to do with the means and resources by which it renews itself, especially as it faces a wide range of challenges to its existence. Important signs are the proliferation of scholarly associations and academies; heightened standards for identifying genuine authority; liveliness of debate in the society, or the umma, or the sangha, or the ecclesia in general; the development of subtle and elaborate ritual; increasing achievement in artistic expression of all kinds. Most important is that they have a collective focus on the mysteries that lie at their core, mysteries they are neither able to resolve nor to abandon. What provides Islam its vitality, for example, is not just that Muslims find the Quran still endlessly interpretable, but that they cannot stop interpreting. It is not something that, being not yet adequately understood, they can set aside. It presents them with a series of questions they deeply need to answer, *and* they need others to join them in the quest. Even more, as they come together to resolve these unknowns, the greater and the more imponderable they become—and the more irresistible. Suppose, however, that

Muslims come to a broad consensus on how the Quran is to be interpreted; were they to do so, they would have substituted the consensus for the text itself. The Quran would then have become dispensable. At best it would serve as a proof text for one or another of their beliefs. (In fact, it is the beliefs that prove the meanings of the text.) On the other hand, the text would become just as dispensable were Muslims simply to have lost their curiosity about its meanings. It would be a mere historical oddity like the Egyptian Book of the Dead or the Code of Hammurabi.

Note that none of this has to do with belief, or truth, or views of the world as such. Religion, understood in this way, is not a catalogue of assertions subject to evaluation and correction by nonparticipants in the *communitas*. Its essential writings are endlessly interpretable, resisting any kind of summary or translation into the language of "outsiders"—and "insiders." Muslims insist that the Quran, to be understood, cannot be translated from the Arabic. In fact, it cannot be translated at all, even into Arabic. It remains permanently above all definitive restatement, regardless of its language. Its full meanings are as hidden from Muslims as they are from others.

Still, assigning the word "religion" to any human phenomenon must be tentative. What can be said is that elements of religion are present, even if all but undetectable, in every expression of *communitas*. And even at its highest level, religion is never free of the causes of its undoing. What holds a family together over a generation or more is certainly more than blood or economic dependence or even shared values; it is ultimately something the family itself can never fully grasp. To this degree it has an element of religiousness. At the other end, no community of saints or spiritual masters or inspired teachers is free of the in-cipient belief systems that threaten their heightened religiosity. Religions die. If the "great" religions have thrived for mil-lennia, their identities remarkably intact, it is no guarantee that they have millennia still to go, or even decades, or less. Egyptian religion (though whether *communitas* or *civitas* is debatable) came to an abrupt end after an existence of more than three thousand years when Alexander conquered it in the fourth century, re-placing it with the Ptolemaic dynasty that ended three centuries later (with the suicide of Cleopatra, its thirteenth monarch). The many expired religions of Central and South America, though of uncertain length, generally spanned centuries with only modest change. Navajos, Maoris, Hittites, Mithraists, Taghkanics, and Crees had extensive periods of stability, and while traces of their ancient traditions can be identified, their mortality is certain.

The reasons religions die are many, and we may not always know what they are. We can speculate. Some are simply con-quered and their populations crushed (Aztecs, Seminoles). The disappearance of others eludes explanation (Mayans, Anasazi). Some were slowly absorbed by other traditions (Confucianism, Gnosticism), or followed such severe disciplines that they ex-hausted themselves (Essenes, Mithraists, Shakers), or evolved so extensively from their original form that they gave away their uniqueness (Taoism, the Celts). If there is any generalization that covers them all, it can be only that by one way or another they lost their identity when they identified *with* something out-side themselves: a geographic area (Easter Islanders), a political realm (Egyptians), a particular philosophy (Gnostics), an ethnic community (Celts).

What is more relevant here is that, especially in the Age of Faith II, we have seen religions dissolve into networks of belief systems. This is not new. All of the great religions have spun off a wide variety of ideologies. This happens anytime the religious *communitas* identifies with the *civitas* in which it has its home and takes up one of its ideologies as its own. Hinduism regularly blindered itself from its intense and universally accessible spirituality, including the principle of nonviolence, or *ahimsa*, to attach to the despotic rule of emperors and such societal practices as the caste system. Christianity's long flirtation and occasional marriage to the political order has had little trouble finding that its identification with empire—Roman, English, Belgian, Spanish, American—can be backed by justifying theologies. Countless Muslims have never abandoned their dream of a world ruled by a unified caliphate, and in the meantime push to establish sharia, or religious law, as the civil law of a nation. Buddhism and Judaism, on the other hand, though having their moments of ideological fervor, have never significantly given themselves over to *civitas*. Judaism in particular, without a country, a governing institution, a unified culture, a pure ethnic identity, an army, a creed, or a priesthood, is unequaled among religions for the continuity of its *communitas*—a religion that has perfected the art of disagreement, of sustaining arguments of undiminished energy extending across centuries. Jews have established a *civitas* in Israel, but by declaring it to be both a secular and a Jewish state have entered boldly into the subtle problem of combining *civitas* and *communitas* without confusing one with the other. It is not easy.

Although Judaism and Buddhism have never given themselves completely over to *civitas*, it is obvious that some degree of *civitas* is necessary for every religion. There must be social environments stable enough to sustain its poets, especially those who can see beyond the boundaries that make their vision possible. The ideal *civitas* is one that nourishes the broadest possible range of disagreement with itself. This is Christianity's strongest feature: it tirelessly provokes its members to object to prevailing doctrines without having to abandon the faith. It is true that over the centuries it has often presented its doctrines as beliefs. As *doctrines*, or teachings, they depend for their effectiveness on the presence of students who will challenge and improve them. As *beliefs*, they depend on complicit listeners who adopt them without resistance, and do not exceed the prescribed limit of interpretation. But neither Christianity nor any of the great religions has ever been able to successfully erect barriers against the dreaded barbarian incursions of fresh ideas. Their orthodoxies, for all the systematic and comprehensive order with which they are offered, throw too thin a cover over the recurring Christian fascination with its central mystery: the "real" Jesus, the best and least known person who ever lived. So far, all their rationally assembled dogmatic schemes have been greeted with more learned ignorance than obedience. So far. But once this precarious balance tips one way or the other, the religion begins to die: its thought is too restricted, or too unrestricted, to be thought at all.

Christianity, for all its durability and explosive growth, is showing early signs of mortality. By splintering into an array of factions, lining up behind political leaders and their ideologies, adopting local mores, and identifying with ethnic communities, it seems to be losing the balance between *communitas* and *civitas*.

The fracturing that began with Luther has become extreme: denominations are weakening, the number of sects is growing, along with megachurches that have no connection to larger ecclesiastical bodies. Even more perilous, this splintering seems to have tossed aside the centuries of culture that has accumulated around the historic church—its music, literature, architecture, rituals, schools of higher (nonideological) learning. The grand conversation that provided the unity for the religion as a whole is largely ignored. In short, Christianity is losing its resonance. Its history looks to be a matter more of decades than millennia. It is less a religion than a collection of belief systems. Where are its poets?

It must be emphasized that the poets (*poietai*) are often much more disturbing than they are comforting or amusing. If the genius of poetry is to introduce horizonal vision into our carefully designed and ordered view of the world, the recognition that our boundaries are merely arbitrary can be deeply unsettling. Before the Civil War, Lincoln regarded the existence of the Union to be as fixed as a law of nature. It was a boundary he did not hesitate to defend by leading the nation into a bloody war with itself. By its end, however, the poet rose above the politician. The Second Inaugural, far from being a celebration of victory, is an admission of national culpability: we ascribed to ourselves an authority we do not properly have. Lincoln takes his place in a long march of those poets who expose us to our deepest self-contradictions. The prophets of Israel attacked the injustice of rulers no less than the easy piety of the religious. "I hate, I despise your festivals, and I take no delight in your solemn assemblies" (Amos 5:21). The unknown poet of the book of Job draws even religion itself into question. Having declared he had lived an exemplary life—not abused his slaves, for example, not looked at a virgin, not sought after gold—he challenges God to explain his suffering. Out of a whirlwind, God calls back, "I shall question you, and you shall declare to me. Were you there when I laid the foundations of the earth?" (38:3–4, a difficult passage for creationists). It is as much as saying that Job has not the least understanding of who God is or what he is about. In the gospel of John, Jesus is said to declare, "The truth will set you free." This Jesus, however, is as plainly wrong as the prewar Lincoln. It is the shared assumption that we have the truth that is so devastating to every form of *communitas.* Better he had said, "What will set you free is not truth but *truthfulness,*" an open and frank exchange of divergent views. Indeed, elsewhere in the gospels Jesus does not proclaim the truth so much as to confound every attempt to possess it. His poetic journey across Palestine, teaching and healing, was greeted by far more consternation and puzzlement than reassurance and clarity—even by his own disciples. It was his poetry, not his army, that the Roman *civitas* attempted to kill. Socrates died for the same reason; he was "corrupting" the youth of Athens by teaching them to wonder about everything.

The question remains: if religion is at its core so antithetical to belief, why does it happen that belief systems gather so persistently around genuine religious expression? Recent critics of religion may have been mistaken in thinking that it was religion they were attacking and not the isolated beliefs with which they mistakenly identified them, but they have a point, inasmuch as believers do regularly represent themselves as truly religious—or impute to their beliefs an aura of pseudo-religious validation.

Put another way, we might ask, *What is it about religion that causes believers to reject it?* Why are some Christians so certain in their understanding of the resurrection of Jesus, or Muslims so convinced that the Quran justifies a violent form of jihad, when it should be perfectly obvious to both that these are issues that have been unresolved after centuries of animated and learned debate?

Any answer to this curious fact must be speculative at best. We can at least say that whenever we turn to religion for answers to the questions that press all of us for our simply being human (what happens at death? why is there evil? where did it all come from? how will it end? why is there something rather than nothing?), instead of answers we are offered a deepened expression of the same question. When the dying Buddha assured his grieving friends that his body would decay like any other earthly object, he was asked whether he would live on after death. He answered in effect: we cannot say the Buddha lives on; we cannot say he does not; we cannot say he both lives on and does not; we cannot say he neither lives on nor does not. On the one hand, he emphasizes the reality of his death, on the other, the utter impossibility of understanding it. This open-ended, or what I have called horizonal, way of thinking then penetrates every aspect of Buddhism. It cancels the claim that anyone, even the most accomplished Buddhists, or bodhisattvas, can say what Buddhism is truly about.

By virtue of the ignorance inherent in its long conversation with itself, each religion can behold another only with wonder. That they are rivals, or that they have contradictory views of God, or that they cannot exist in the same time and place, or that one endangers the other—none of this comes to mind among the religious. The great danger of belief systems is that the opposing sides are sure they *do* understand each other. When Christians fault the Muslim idea of God, calling Islam a false deity or a satanic creation, they have done more than reveal their flawed understanding of Islam, they have severed themselves from their own faith. They are no longer Christians, but willfully ignorant ideologues.

Far from providing false or unverifiable answers to our questions, the religions provide no answers at all. On this basis, one explanation for the proliferation of belief systems at the edges of the great religions is that they provide a shield against this absolute openness, a protection in advance against what might lie just beyond the horizon and so far unseen, or even imaginable. Believers, in short, are terrified by genuine expressions of religion, and respond to them by vigorously ignoring them. They take refuge in agreement, solidarity of membership, and the sense that they belong to something that exists independently of their participation in it. Thus it was when Urban II saw a loss of fervor in Christendom, he initiated in the year 1095 what was to become several centuries of costly, savage, and ultimately failed crusades against the Saracens. It was far more reassuring for medieval Christians to battle Islam than it was for them to inquire unrestrictedly into the learned and thriving Islamic civilization. In the meantime, of course, it was a way of escaping any inquiry into the great uncertainties of Christianity itself. As much as it was a declared war against infidels, it was an undeclared war against their own poets.

The poets, of course, are not at war with believers. They do not meet the authority of sword and crown with armies of their own, but only, like Galileo, with a continuing attempt to reimagine the universe. And like Galileo, they are easily brushed aside by the powerful. Those who share their vision are small in number compared to the masses attracted to belief systems in general. Without their disturbing presence in the *communitas*, however, the *communitas* loses its integrity and if it survives at all it is by surrendering its authority to the *civitas*. As a result, the *civitas* itself will become hollow and brittle, finally sharing the fate of Soviet Marxism, or Italian fascism, or Argentine despotism, or American exclusivism.

In laying out the religious case against belief, it may seem that I have privileged the former over the latter. It must be said, however, although I can offer no statistical basis for it, that the world is far more attracted to belief systems than to religion as I have described it. Nonetheless, poets will always rise in their midst, even in the most severe, knowing they lack every form of worldly power, hoping only that their singing will outlast them. But if it does, even if it is long remembered, finally there is only oblivion. Why then do they continue to sing? They have no choice. They know they are ignorant.

CODA

The question inevitably arises as to whether this proposal of a religious case against belief is not itself a belief system. Of course it is. The very title indicates that something is to be opposed, that there are exclusive and competitive, even combative, points of view at work throughout the discussion. To make a case against something, anything at all, is a sure sign that there is bound to be a collision of belief systems. (After all, have I not asserted that belief is always belief *against* a matching disbelief?) What I have intended to present here is a coherent argument against what I consider to be a distorted understanding of the nature of religion. The simple point is that to attack one or another "religious" belief, as if it were an attack on religion itself, is not only embarrassingly ignorant, it bypasses a far more searing critique that comes from within the religions themselves. There is no question that the kinds of believers we are concerned with here have sponsored unconscionable violence over the ages, and especially over the last century. The question is how to understand why this might be so and how most effectively to address the issue. To say simply that they are *wrong* widely misses the point. There is only one defense for the apparent contradiction of dismissing belief systems by way of another belief system, as I have done: the argument presented in these pages must provide the basis for its own rejection. Indeed, by citing the importance of disagreement to a vital and ongoing conversation is all but to beg for a critique of this critique. I am not initiating a conversation but joining one, in this case one that has been dazzlingly under way for millennia. Any thought that I might bring it all to an end satisfactory to myself, or anyone else, is hilarious at best. My aim is the opposite: to add a voice that, if it is effective at all, will only raise other voices. And the more clamorous the response the better.

ACKNOWLEDGMENTS

The first public exposure of the ideas in the book was to a puzzled lay audience at a memorial colloquium for the theologian and college president Harry Smith, in Chapel Hill, North Carolina. The modified argument then received a clamorous professional reception at a meeting of the New Haven Theological Group. Carol Mack caught crucial errors in an early version. My agent, Lynn Nesbit, as always, displayed her noted skill at protecting art from commercial compromise. Ann Godoff and Lindsay Whalen were the very models of editorial scrutiny and advice. The book is substantially different and much improved from the manuscript they first read. Tom Driver was unrestrained in his critical review of the book's intellectual content, and relentless in his repeated demands for greater clarity and accuracy. It was a high challenge I fear was not fully met.

NOTES

PART I BELIEF

1. James Reston Jr., *Galileo: A Life* (New York: HarperCollins, 1998), p. 261.

2. Nicholas of Cusa, *De Docta Ignorantia*, tr. Jasper Hopkins (Minneapolis: A. J. Banning Press, 1990), I, 1, 10, pp. 52ff.

3. *Three Plays by Thornton Wilder* (New York: HarperCollins, 1961), p. 28.

4. Wallace Hooper, "Inertial Problems in Galileo's Preinertial Framework," in Peter Machamer, ed., *The Complete Companion to Galileo* (Cambridge, MA: Cambridge University Press, 1998), p. 147.

5. Giorgiode Santillana, *The Crime of Galileo* (Chicago, 1955), p. 186.

6. It is impossible to give the exact number of the Crusades; it was a nearly nonstop activity that continued to the end of the fifteenth century.

7. Newt Gingrich, *Winning the Future: A 21st Century Contract with America* (Washington, DC: Regnery, 2005), pp. 43ff.

8. See especially David Barton, *Original Intent: The Courts, the Constitution, and Religion* (Aledo, TX: WallBuilders, 2004).

9. Sam Harris, *The End of Faith: Religion, Terror, and the Future of Reason* (New York: W. W. Norton, 2004).

10. Ibid., p. 221.

11. Ibid., p. 110.

12. Ibid., p. 123.

13. Ibid., p. 225.

14. Ibid., p. 224.

15. Daniel C. Dennett, *Breaking the Spell* (New York: Viking, 2006).

16. Quoted in Roland H. Bainton, *Here I Stand: A Life of Martin Luther* (New York: Abbingdon-Cokesbury Press, 1950), p. 179.

17. The latter half of the statement was never recorded in the proceedings of the trial but has been so frequently quoted that it has the weight of authenticity.

18. Quoted in Bainton, p. 189.

19. Ibid., p. 163.

20. Ibid., p. 223.

21. Scholars commonly distinguish between the "early Luther" and Luther in his mature, later writings when his thinking seems to harden into something near dogma, an ironic echo of the kind of Catholicism he initially rejected.

22. It is worth a footnote to record a suggestive act of Charles. Some years after his encounter with Luther, apparently exhausted by the burdens of his office, or disturbed by the unrestricted use of power, he surrendered most of the empire to one of his sons and spent the last two years of his life as a simple monk in a Spanish monastery.

23. Acts, 9:3–4.

24. *Confessions*, tr. Garry Wills (New York: Penguin Press, 2006), pp. 185ff.

25. Wilson H. Kimnach, Kenneth P. Minkema, and Douglas A. Sweeney, eds., *The Sermons of Jonathan Edwards* (New Haven: Yale University Press, 1999), pp. 65, 50, 43.

26. It is common for advocates of intelligent design to represent their views as equivalent to science. In the popular creationist book *Grand Canyon: A Different View* (Green Forest, AR, 2005), author Tom Vail asserts that "both humanism and evolution are as much a religion as Christianity. They are all systems of belief" (p. 9). On the other hand, Michael J. Behe, prolific defender of intelligent design, when asked if it was based on religious beliefs said, "No, it isn't. It is based entirely on observable, physical evidence from nature." *New York Times*, October 18, 2005, p. A14.

27. In their massive five-volume *Creeds and Confessions of Faith in the Christian Church* (New Haven: Yale University Press, 2003), Jaroslav Pelikan and Valerie Hotchkiss have collected 211 major creeds, omitting scores of minor efforts.

28. I am indebted to Ronald C. White's *Lincoln's Greatest Speech: The Second Inaugural* (New York: Simon & Schuster, 2002) for a detailed description of the setting as well as parts of his analysis of the address itself. The italics are Lincoln's.

29. *The Portable Plato*, tr. Benjamin Jowett (New York: Viking, 1957), pp. 674, 676.

PART II RELIGION

1. *Antiquities of the Jews*, 18.3.3.

2. The only other first-century reference was made by the Roman historian Suetonius, who, writing around the middle of the century, named as a troublemaker a certain "Chrestos."

3. However, the dating of all events in the ancient world, before the invention of calendars, is notoriously imprecise. From the gospel accounts, for example, Jesus's death could have occurred anywhere between 29 and 31. See E. P. Sanders, *The Historical Figure of Jesus* (London: Penguin Books, 1993), pp. 282ff.

4. See Frank Peters, *The Voice, the Word, the Book* (Princeton, NJ: Princeton University Press, 2007), pp. 108ff.

5. Although, strangely, elsewhere in John's gospel Jesus is serenely unmoved by the events around him. Even his trial was "without anxiety or suspense, a crucifixion without suffering and without pathos." Paula Fredriksen, *From Jesus to Christ* (New Haven: Yale University Press, 1988), p. 23.

6. See Sanders, *The Historical Figure of Jesus*, pp. 276ff.

7. Paula Fredriksen's stunning volume *From Jesus to Christ* provides a useful summary of the highly varied images of Jesus that appear in the four gospels and the letters of Paul. See especially her chapter 3, pp. 18–64. The remainder of her book is a deft scholarly examination of Jesus as he was understood in the Hellenistic and Jewish context of the first century.

8. He did, however, undertake to make sense of the trinity (God the Father, Son, and Holy Spirit) in his large volume *De Trinitate*. But it did little to end the issue. Bitter debates raged for centuries afterward.

9. Irenaeus took the principle of *recapitulation* so far that he had Jesus living into old age as did Adam, even citing a witness who claimed to see Jesus wandering as an old man in a distant land. *Against Heresies*, Book II, 22, 5.

10. *A Scholastic Miscellany: Anselm to Ockham*, tr. Eugene R. Fairweather (Philadelphia: Westminster, 1956), p. 100.

11. Ibid., p. 110.

12. Ibid., p. 137.

13. Ibid., p. 151.

14. See Gordon E. Michalson, *Lessing's "Ugly Ditch"* (University Park, PA: Pennsylvania State University Press, 1985).

15. Immanuel Kant, *Religion Within the Boundaries of Mere Reason and Other Writings*, trs. Allen Wood and George di Giovanni (New York: Columbia University Press, 1998).

16. Described in Stephen Prothero's *American Jesus* (New York: Farrar, Straus, and Giroux, 2003), pp. 19ff.

17. *Kierkegaard's Concluding Unscientific Postscript*, tr. David F. Swenson and Walter Lowrie (Princeton, NJ: Princeton University Press, 1941), p. 182. (Kierkegaard's italics.)

18. *Geschichte der Leben-Jesu-Faschung* (Tübingen, Germany: J. C. B. Mohr, 1913), p. 642.

19. Walter Rauschenbusch was one of the founding members and the principal thinker of a loosely organized movement known as the "Social Gospel." He saw Jesus above all else as a social reformer, but a reformer not merely interested in rearranging societal institutions but in the salvation of humanity. "The fundamental first step in the salvation of mankind was the achievement of the personality of Jesus. Within him the Kingdom of God got its first foothold in humanity." The kingdom is not to be confused with the church, which has become a conservative institution interested only in its own prosperity. The reforms Rauschenbusch envisioned had a striking similarity to the goals of nineteenth-century socialists. *A Theology for the Social Gospel* (New York: Macmillan, 1917), p. 151.

20. In a handsome volume of photographs and text, *In Grand Canyon: A Different View* (Green Forest, AR, 2005), author Tom Vail makes the classic "creationist" claim that, according to the "inerrant Word of God," the world was not only made in six (twenty-four-hour) days, but that about fifteen hundred years later (forty-five hundred years ago?) a flood covered the earth, creating such phenomena as the Grand Canyon.

21. Rudolf Bultmann, under the influence of existentialism, and repelled by Barth's biblicism, argued that the New Testament description of Jesus is so infused with the mythology of the Mediterranean world of the time that the events related are completely unintelligible to the scientifically oriented mod-

ern age. The three-tiered universe, the virgin birth, the miracles of healing are all unbelievable to contemporary intelligence. The New Testament account of Jesus must then be "demythologized." When it is, very little is left, but enough to see that Jesus's relation to himself challenges us to confront the issue of our own existence, especially the fact that we are mysterious to ourselves and morally responsible for all our actions. Bultmann goes so far as to say that even if we could somehow prove that Jesus actually rose from the grave, it would be meaningless to issues of faith. The principal issue has to do with what he calls our "inauthenticity," or not being truly "who" we are. See especially *Kerygma and Myth,* tr. Reginald Fuller (London: S.P.C.K. Press, 1953).

22. The hit musical *Jesus Christ Superstar* was written by Andrew Lloyd Webber and Tim Rice, opening on Broadway in 1971. Before the year was out, the record had sold three million copies. See Prothero, *American Jesus,* pp. 132ff.

23. *Nazional Sozialismus.*

24. Joseph Smith's Book of Mormon was written down by friends as he dictated it, reading from the golden leaves of a hidden book whose existence was revealed by the angel Moroni. In his early twenties, Smith published the translations, which tell the story of a small body of Israelites who make their way across the Pacific to Central America, about four hundred years before the birth of Jesus in Palestine. After his resurrection, Jesus appeared to the remnants of this American civilization, preaching to them much in the style of the New Testament, but with a great number of teachings not found there. Nonetheless, from the beginning, "Latter-Day Saints have considered themselves Christian, claiming their religion to be the most authentic form of Bible Christianity in existence." Although Mormons regard themselves as Christians, it is nearly impossible to find Christians who recognize the Jesus described in the Book of Mormon and therefore consider themselves also to be Mormons. Still, for all his novelty, it is not to be denied that the Mormon Jesus has stirred a movement of millions around the globe and continues to do so with no sign of abating. See Claudia Lauper Bushman and Richard Lyman Bushman, *Building the Kingdom: A History of Mormons in America* (New York: Oxford University Press, 1999), p. x. The most compendious modern history of Mormonism is Terryl L. Givens's *By the Hand of Mormon: The American Scripture that Launched a New World Religion* (New York: Oxford University Press, 2002).

25. Quoted by Stephen Prothero, *American Jesus,* p. 215.

26. From Bruce Barton's enormously popular book *The Man Nobody Knows* (Indianapolis: Bobbs-Merrill, 1925): Jesus was "an outdoor man whom our modern thought most admires; and the vigorous activities of his days gave his nerves the strength of steel." He was "broad shouldered" (p. 52). He had the gift of picking the right men to form his "organization." Barton, an advertising executive himself, adds that "every one of the 'principles of modern salesmanship' on which businessmen so much pride themselves, are brilliantly exemplified in Jesus' life and work" (p. 104).

27. "Intelligent design" is a term describing a large, loose body of speculation on the creation of the universe as it exists, taking special note of the number of the improbable coincidental elements that make it possible—in fact, make it necessarily what it is. It poses as a direct opposite of the Darwinian view that evolution is an accidental occurrence.

28. The sensational best seller, Hal Lindsey's *The Late Great Planet Earth* (Grand Rapids, MI: Zondervan, 1970).

29. The Jesus Seminar, an association of about two hundred biblical scholars, or "fellows," founded by Robert Funk in 1985, is the first group to engage in a collective effort to find the most authentic words and acts of Jesus by way of modern principles of textual interpretation. Their signal publication is *The Five Gospels: The Search for the Authentic Words of Jesus*, tr. Robert Funk, Roy W. Hoover, and the Jesus Seminar (New York: Macmillan, 1993), a collaboration of the fellows who literally voted on the possible authenticity of each verse in the New Testament. The Jesus Seminar, for all its deliberative care and intelligence, has been savagely attacked by nonparticipating scholars. See especially Luke Timothy Johnson, *The Real Jesus: The Misguided Quest for the Historical Jesus and the Truth of the Traditional Gospels* (San Francisco: Harper One, 1996). After a vituperative scorching of the Jesus Seminar, Johnson proposes a Jesus of his own arrived at by a methodology somewhat different from Funk's, but still a Jesus for the most part unique to Johnson himself. (Note the title.)

30. The painting by Warner Sallman, *Head of Christ*, that hangs prominently in thousands of church meeting rooms, pastors' offices, and homes.

31. John Dominic Crossan, *The Historical Jesus: The Life of a Mediterranean Peasant* (San Francisco: HarperSanFrancisco, 1992), pp. 421ff. Crossan locates Jesus in a rural form of the Cynical life, a philosophy that rejects the formal structures of society along with all its hypocrisy and injustice, but does so "practically" by living without possession and property.

32. See Harvey Cox, *Fire from Heaven: The Rise of Pentecostal Spirituality and the Reshaping of Religion in the Twenty-first Century* (Reading, PA: Addison-Wesley, 1995).

33. The New York Public Library lists more than five hundred books on the subject of Liberation Theology. See especially the publications of Orbis Press.

34. Tim LaHaye and Jerry B. Jenkins, *Glorious Appearing: The End of Days* (Wheaton, IL: Tyndale House, 2004), is (apparently) the last of a series of twelve "Left Behind" books, telling the story of the final battle at Armageddon. At the conclusion, Jesus casts the generals of the army of Satan "howling and screeching" into a "yawning chasm" that closes behind them (p. 380).

35. The Jesus evoked in countless presidential addresses.

36. The word derives from the Latin root for "to bind." This is linguistically very suggestive when we consider that the Sanskrit "yoga" has a somewhat similar meaning, evident in the English derivative "yoke." Is it going too far to consider all religions separate yogic disciplines, or ways to unify otherwise disconnected phenomena? If so, this does not in the least imply that they are all variations of the same phenomenon, any more than kundalini yoga is interchangeable with Zen Buddhist modes of meditation.

37. Mahatma Gandhi, *All Religions Are True* (Bombay: Baratiya Vidya Bhavan, 1962), pp. 4ff.

38. Edward Tylor in his *Primitive Culture* (London: Routledge, 1994) says simply, "It seems best . . . simply to claim as a minimum definition of Religion, the belief in Spiritual Beings" (p. 424). The great sociologist Emile Durkheim calls religion "a unified system of beliefs and practices relative to sacred things,

that is to say, things set apart and forbidden—beliefs and practices which unite in one single moral community called a Church, all those who adhere to them." *The Elementary Forms of Religious Life I* (New York: Free Press, 1995), p. 47. For a more contemporary effort, see Henry Rosemont Jr., *Rationality and Religious Experience: The Continuing Relevance of the World's Spiritual Traditions* (New York: Columbia University Press, 2001). A prominent place on this list must be saved for Mircea Eliade; see especially his *Patterns in Comparative Religion* (New York, 1958).

39. A. N. Whitehead, *Religion in the Making* (New York: Macmillan, 1927).

40. Rudolf Otto, tr. John Harvey, *Idea of the Holy* (Oxford: Oxford University Press, 1928).

41. Paul Tillich, *The Courage to Be* (New Haven: Yale University Press, 1953).

42. Jonathan Z. Smith, "In Comparison a Magic Still Dwells," reprinted in Kimberley C. Patton and Benjamin C. Ray, eds., *A Magic Still Dwells: Comparative Religion in the Postmodern Age* (Berkeley: University of California Press, 2000).

43. It is a staple of postmodern thought that difference as it is understood here should be regarded as *différence*, using the French word to make the point that there is no way of reconciling the two. The "gap" cannot be crossed. Smith's essay and those of the respondents reject that extreme view.

44. Smith, "In Comparison a Magic Still Dwells," p. 41.

45. Readers familiar with my *Finite and Infinite Games* will note that I have interpreted religion as a form of the infinite game—though an imperfect form, each religion imperfect in its own way. A finite game is defined there as a game one plays to win; an infinite as a game played to keep playing. The imperfections of each religion are understood as the entrance of *finite* players into the infinite game, bringing with them the intention of winning their conflicts instead of keeping them alive, thereby ending the game to their own presumed gain. The burden on *infinite* players is to find a way of integrating what is interruptive into what is ongoing. Although ultimately there can be only one infinite game, it is all but unthinkable that it will ever be achieved. Until it is achieved, even long-enduring institutions like the great religions will remain opaque to each other, and are doomed to fail, eventually slipping back into belief systems (that is, finite games).

PART III   RELIGION BEYOND BELIEF

1. See especially Otto Rank, *The Myth of the Birth of the Hero* (Baltimore: Johns Hopkins University Press, 2004); Joseph Campbell, *The Hero with a Thousand Faces* (Princeton, NJ: Princeton University Press, 1968); Erich Neumann, *The Origins and History of Consciousness* (New York: Pantheon, 1954).

2. As comprehensive as the U.S. Constitution is, it is inconceivable that there will come a time when it will never need another amendment or extensive interpretation.

INDEX

ABOUT THE AUTHOR

James P. Carse is Professor Emeritus of Religion at New York University, where for thirty years he directed the Religious Studies Program. His previous books include *The Silence of God, Finite and Infinite Games*, and *Breakfast at the Victory*. He lives in New York City.